Praise for *My Dear Comrades*

"Sunu Chandy's *My Dear Comrades* thriv   space in which politics and personal story connect. Here, each experience pulls the weight of its complicated history; each observation is viewed through the lens of a social justice warrior, but also through a guide leading us toward enlightenment and empathy. Chandy's poems burst with an empowering energy that's unshakable, unstoppable."

- Rigoberto González, author of five poetry collections including *The Book of Ruin*

"In Sunu Chandy's *My Dear Comrades*, she turns her exquisite attention toward everyday rituals of violence, indoctrination, and subjugation. Over and over, she interrogates some of our most-metabolized rituals, denying them the safety of invisibility, as when she writes: 'Years later, during the middle of law school, I learned this rule by observation: We must stand when the judge enters the courtroom.' And then later: 'In that moment I learned much of what I needed to know about the law.' At the heart of her refusal is a poetics and an ethics of discipline, tenderness, and attention that reminds me of the work of Martín Espada and Audre Lorde. My Dear Comrades is a stunningly lucid and deeply personal work about law and power, race and queerness. Love."

- Aracelis Girmay, author of *the black maria* and *kingdom animalia*

"At the foundation of *My Dear Comrades* is a belief in the strength of community, whether that is intimate family, a wider chosen community or a geographically determined 'general public.' Each kind of community deserves—requires—the same kind of care. The attentions these poems give is indeed intimate but their intention and embrace is wide and public. Sunu Chandy is a generous poet, wise and willful and fierce and kind."

- Kazim Ali, author of several books including most recently, *The Voice of Sheila Chandra* and *Northern Light*

"Sunu Chandy's debut collection *My Dear Comrades* is a love letter to the creation of community, queer family building, and fighting against injustice. In language that both challenges and consoles, Chandy investigates, as in the poem 'Calculate,' '[w]ords that can build us / up or tear us to shreds...' This book looks closely at language, questioning who owns it, who silences it, and what silence protects. Chandy asks: how do we repair our broken world? And the poems answer, in a brilliant call for social justice, workers' rights, new constructions of family and most of all, deep compassion."

- Nicole Cooley, author of *Breach, Girl After Girl After Girl,* and *Of Marriage*

"From the love underpinning LGBTQ adoption to the struggles of immigration, this lyrically inclusive and politically unifying debut collection makes the best and most beautiful argument toward belonging."

-Roger Sedarat, author of *Ghazal Games* and *Haji as Puppet: an Orientalist Burlesque*

"*My Dear Comrades* lives at the intersection of the personal and the political. Fearlessly, with candor and grace, these poems bear witness, shatter oppressive silences, and call injustice by its many names. At the same time, they acknowledge the complicated matrices that make us human—our relationships, desires, the gnarled pathways of the heart. Bracing and compassionate, fortifying and vulnerable, Chandy debuts here as a necessary voice that reminds us: 'Remember integrity. / Remember what is at stake.'"

-Lauren K. Alleyne, author of *Difficult Fruit* and *Honeyfish*

"Sunu Chandy's *My Dear Comrades* considers the multiple boundaries and borders that the poet crosses into justice: political, social, and the deeply interior. In sure language Chandy shows her own path towards her personal ethics as a mother, a queer daughter, an activated empath searching for a deep love that transforms as it creates community. I have been thirsty for a poetry that demonstrates fierce allyship and what it means for queers of color living in the United States. *My Dear Comrades* is a map into the heart's country that abolished borders. Indeed, this collection proceeds from a damaged and flawed world and forges a complicated, abounding beauty."

-Rajiv Mohabir, author of *Cutlish and Antiman: A Hybrid Memoir*

"Sunu Chandy's poems are evocations of how we build bonds and resemblance, how we live in community, how we work towards justice. With courage and commitment, *My Dear Comrades* breaks open the details of life—queer romance, city living, family gatherings, adoption processes, legal document review—to investigate the possibilities and power of practices of repair, rebuilding, forgiveness, compassion, and justice. These poems are rituals of rearrangement: Chandy shows us how to build and rebuild relationships, cities, gender, labor, and our relationships to ourselves so that we can collectively offer a 'footstep/towards something possible.' *My Dear Comrades* is an invitation into community, into possibility, into the work of justice."

-Purvi Shah, author of *Miracle Marks* and *Terrain Tracks*

"Sunu Chandy's poems are miniature stories: sensual flashes, immersive scenes in which whole lives are glimpsed and revealed. Flatbush, Jerusalem, Kingston, Kerala, and more: In close quarters and intimate spaces, the speaker of the poem sits on the floor or breaks bread while keenly observing how power moves through and within the people she encounters. Rituals of justice and resistance wend their way through moments of grief and care. The book is wide-ranging in its subjects, but ultimately it is family, given and chosen, that forms the tender, beating heart of this beautiful collection."

- Minal Hajratwala, author of *Leaving India: My Family's Journey from Five Villages to Five Continents and Bountiful Instructions for Enlightenment;* Founder of Camp Unicorn

"Sunu Chandy's debut poetry collection, *My Dear Comrades*, is relentless in its ability to speak truth to power. Readers travel along this poetic journey with Chandy as she documents injustices, reflects on her past, and gives us a glimpse into her own struggles, fears and joys. Chandy's poems are intimate and vulnerable, poems of protest and praise, poems that break us and bring us delight. She embraces the complicated and exquisite parts of herself and we are left better for it. The silences in Chandy's poems often speak volumes. When the relative of a friend sexually harasses the narrator, Chandy uses sparse descriptions to frame a disturbing, yet familiar scene: 'It was not dark. It was not night. I was not outside. I was not alone. I was not with strangers. There were women in the vicinity.' In 'Too Pretty,' Chandy's effective use of repetition captures the narrator's fears for herself, a queer woman of color, along with her genuine concern for queer pre-teens during a homophobic incident on a NYC subway. She closes the poem with a heartfelt silent wish/prayer, 'You all sitting there, laughing laughing/ sitting there on your sixth grade girlfriend's lap/ so free and easy, laughing laughing,/ be safe my handsome girls, be safe my pretty boys.' Many of her poems evoke the powerful political poetry of Margaret Walker and Pat Parker, such as 'Shelter-In-Place.' Here, Chandy defiantly affirms 'I pledge allegiance to facing conflict head-on/and choosing our battles./ I pledge allegiance to the organizers,/ to the ones moving through the tears, to people sitting around /a table and writing our poems anyway.' This political praise poem ignites the page; words become a mantra invoking the power of both organizers and poets. Ultimately, *My Dear Comrades*, uplifts and centers the compelling voice of Sunu Chandy, a queer woman of color, whose dedication to community, social justice activism and family center this stunning collection."

-J.P. Howard, author of *Say/Mirror, bury your love poems here, Praise This Complicated Herstory: Legacy, Healing & Revolutionary Poems* and co-editor of *Sinister Wisdom's Black Lesbians—We Are the Revolution!*

My Dear Comrades is a collection of fierce hymns to guide us through those daily atrocities, that seem benign, yet haunt us. Chandy profoundly feels every blow of social injustice, and rather than rage, Chandy hurls sharp wit, pristine imagery, and a cinematic brilliance that takes you through her journey as an immigrant daughter, wife, mother & activist. Chandy shows us how taking in the hard truths in our urbane dailiness crafted with profound self-reflection and metaphor can result in the gorgeous act of rebuilding the human soul. As we navigate our identity in an unprecedented 21st-century global crisis, Chandy shows us that poetry can hold us up."

- Regie Cabico, Split This Rock co-Founder, Poet, Capturing Fire Publisher

"To read Sunu Chandy's *My Dear Comrades* is to participate in a revelation. Through details of chai and military tanks, peppermint soap and broken doorknobs, the poems in Chandy's collection remind us that the smallest moments in life can hold our whole humanity. And isn't this a form of justice, Chandy's poems seem to say, to claim a connected way of being--queer, woman, of color, survivor, parent, spouse, advocate--fully human and vulnerable, awake to both the heartbreaks and the wonders of the world."

-Jen Soriano, author of *Making the Tongue Dry*

"The poems in Sunu Chandy's *My Dear Comrades* sing, shine, shimmer, and slide into our consciousness. They are alive with the everyday and leap to make connections between our personal choices and the direction the world is moving. They remind us that justice is a daily responsibility. And the poems are also deeply personal—funny and heartbreaking in equal measure. Sunu's poems share and praise their origins, discuss their process, and open up conversations within us. They delight, surprise, and complicate at every turn. *My Dear Comrades* should be required reading for anyone who cares about this world."

-Jeffrey Perkins, author of *Kingdom*

"Sunu Chandy's *My Dear Comrades* makes me uncomfortable in the best of ways. She is generous with her personal stories – her path to becoming a parent and mothering, from fertility to adoption to pandemic parenting; her journey to becoming a lawyer, and her never-ending ability to navigate systems that were not built for her, for me, or for so many of us. I'm grateful for the reminder that there can be humor in some of life's toughest moments and sadness in our greatest achievements. And I feel lucky to be one of the comrades on her journey."

-Fatima Goss Graves, President and CEO, National Women's Law Center

"*My Dear Comrades*, a book of poems by Sunu Chandy, is beautifully written, bursting with emotion, heart wrenching, and thought-provoking. I remember feeling hit in the heart in the first few minutes after reading 'Just Act Normal.' I was hooked after that. I recommend checking this out if you love poetry with a purpose."

- Stacey Stevenson, Chief Executive Officer, Family Equality

"Make space in your life to accompany Sunu Chandy as she travels across country, culture, personal experience, and injustices from the merely irritating to the enraging. Feel with your hands the thickly woven tapestries of being: the colors, the heartbreak, the commitment, the joy, the vulnerability, the humanity, the awful harms we humans do each other. It's all threaded together with love: Love of self, of others, of humanity, of justice. Everything, big, small, or in-between is suffused with meaning and the complexity it calls for and deserves. Chandy has a way of capturing our many and varied experiences, and she's laid them down in verse so we can join her and feel our own lives more deeply."

- Lauren R. Taylor, director of Defend Yourself and author of a forthcoming book on empowerment self-defense.

MY DEAR COMRADES

Poems by

Sunu P. Chandy

Regal House Publishing

Published by
Regal House Publishing, LLC
Raleigh, NC 27605
All rights reserved

ISBN -13 (paperback): 9781646033195
ISBN -13 (epub): 9781646033201
Library of Congress Control Number: 2022935696

All efforts were made to determine the copyright holders and obtain their permissions in any circumstance where copyrighted material was used. The publisher apologizes if any errors were made during this process, or if any omissions occurred. If noted, please contact the publisher and all efforts will be made to incorporate permissions in future editions.

Cover design © by C. B. Royal
Cover image © by Ragni Agarwal
Author photo by Fid Thompson

Regal House Publishing, LLC
https://regalhousepublishing.com

Printed in the United States of America

For Satya, for my whole family,
and for all who search for their truth.

We are each other's harvest, we are each other's business,
we are each other's magnitude and bond.

- Gwendolyn Brooks.

Foreword

Sunu P. Chandy's poetry collection *My Dear Comrades* immediately captivated me. The poems strike at the heart and gut level. They move relentlessly through time to weave together first-hand stories of injustice, exclusion, loss, and defeat, but also the power of hope and love, "the footstep/toward something possible". It's rare that I read a group of poems that have such a clear narrative arc, one poem building on another. Suspense, drama, a sense of place, and unforgettable real-life characters all work together here—we become invested in the speaker's story and want to find out what will happen next.

Chandy's worldview is rich, honest and deeply compelling. She engages us tangibly in the experiences of racism, sexism, homophobia, painful loss, marginalization, as well as the sweet complexity of love. She directly portrays the experiences of daily life, along with the characters she interacts with, in vivid, moving, and often humorous language:

The only recent border crossing I can remember
is trying to sneak my 15-year old cousin Jeevan into the studio
audience of *Who Wants to Be a Millionaire*. We had plans B and C
at the ready. Whispering to each other, *Just act
normal*, as the signs *16 and older* kept appearing
on our pathway.

"Just Act Normal"

This is a voice that deserves to be heard and celebrated. I'm delighted to have selected Sunu P. Chandy as the winning recipient of Regal House Publishing's 2021 Terry J. Cox Poetry Award.

Martha Kalin, author of *How to Hold a Flying River*

CONTENTS

ONE

Just Act Normal 3

Divestment... 4

1980 5

Jerusalem 6

Morning, at the Lodge 8

Rolls Royce Quality Factory in China 9

A Good Job for SK....................................... 10

October 11, 2001.. 13

The sticky remnants of packing tape Xs 15

Salvation Army 17

The successful candidate................................ 18

Refused to sign 20

All Rise 22

Onam in Manhattan 26

Diverted 27

Carpe Diem Kombucha 28

Sexism 29

Trueing 30

Too Pretty.. 31

TWO

Sleet 35

Comrades 37

Grade Four Peaches 41

Rebuilding Efforts...................................... 43

International adoption agencies maintain strict rules ... 44

Provenance Unknown 46

Knowledge 47

Kasthaputta Vanhu 49

First Trip to Underhill Park 51

For it has been observed that it takes 20 minutes 53

Fake Help Opening the Fake Ketchup 54

Pausing an Argument 55

Twenty years of Coats 58

Teaching My Daughter To Re-Cap the Toddler Toothpaste . . 60

To Satya, From Satya 61

Impulse Buys 63

Distance Learning 65

Calculate 66

Symmetry 67

Religious, and Spiritual 69

THREE

The Boy in the Holly Berry Store 73

Taxi Driver Brother Man 75

Cracked. 77

Where the Wild Things are 83

Fake Roof Deck Makeovers in Brooklyn 84

Boxing-up the China 85

I grow fond of the kitchen cabinet doors that swing open. . . . 86

Fake Drinking Wells in Kerala 87

Practice raking leaves 88

Apartment 5J 89

Ode to the Broken Printer, Three Printers Ago 90

Radical Love-Building Relationships Workshop 91

Heavy Wash Cycle 93

Rebuilding Efforts II 94

Ninety-Five 96

Mattina Mia 98

Shelter-In-Place 101

Self-Portrait as a Vase of Half-Wilted Flowers 103

First Quarantine Poem 104

Rebuilding Efforts III 106

Gratitude List 108

Third Quarantine Poem 110

Wish 111

Tell us your reason for canceling.* 113

Things I Didn't Know I Loved 115

Write a poem in which you show love. 117

What might happen to your writing if 119

Make Yourself at Home 119

Rearranging the Furniture 124

Notes 127

Acknowledgements 129

Gratitudes 131

ONE

Unauthorized Ice Cream Break

Just Act Normal

The only recent border crossing I can remember
is trying to sneak my 15-year old cousin Jeevan into the studio
audience of *Who Wants to Be a Millionaire*. We had plans B and C
at the ready. Whispering to each other, *Just act
normal*, as the signs *16 and older* kept appearing
on our pathway. Praising his basketball height
we thought we would get away with it. And we did.
What happens though, when it's not an afternoon,
but the rest of your life, and it's not a studio audience,
it's another country. Is Plan B still
to leave one family member behind?
Is Plan C still that Jaya will wait with Jeevan
in Central Park until the end of the show?

Divestment

My first memories of grapes
were not buying them
to support the farmworkers.
At age eight I couldn't quite draw
the connection and wondered,
if we don't buy the grapes,
how would the workers get paid?

This idea of money as politics, as currency,
as movement building, takes some imagination,
some organizing, some dedication
to personal responsibility and community
accountability, together. What money does
in our name alone, small,
but if we get 10 more, 100 more, a dent, a message,
against apartheid, for farmworkers, for Middle-East peace.

Four years of planning culminated
in a meeting with Contractor Joe
on Tuesday evening. The sale on cabinets
ends next weekend. The factory that burned down
in Bangladesh has among its clients, Ikea. The personal
cost became too high. I willed myself
to unread the second half of the news article.
How 'bout we boycott Walmart instead—
        a place we never shop anyway.

1980

It began with an afternoon Easter egg hunt
in Ohio and for four years we never stopped
seeking. The American flag on our parsonage
symbolized failed attempts
at assimilation despite new formalities
documenting citizenship. Hanging my brother's diapers
on the clothesline, my mother's Malayalam rang
jagged through the backyards, and no one danced
with the brown girl whose class picture turned out *pretty*
though, for an Indian. When the yellow Ryder truck arrived
to our one-traffic-light town, I wore my striped purple Izod shirt
for the occasion and waved goodbye
to my three best friends. Relieved
to start junior high elsewhere, in the *gang-infested*
(as they called it) City of Chicago.

Jerusalem

Morning mint tea with Mohammad and then shopping
in the market—today for ceramic blue tiles and an olive
wood nativity set. I weave between tourists
on the Holy Land-Jesus-Way of the Cross tours. Someone
was stabbed right here yesterday. Cries were heard
two streets over at our Gloria Hotel.

I touch the stone where Jesus had once lay, light
a candle and pay my donation. I place yet another prayer
in the Wailing Wall. This time that no one else be
sexually assaulted, ever again, *inshallah*. Our classmate's body
was grabbed on the first night. She still shivers
when she talks about that evening. Last week's prayers,
the classmate who vomits at the hotel, after dinner, every night.

We tour refugee camps with starving children, and then harvest
lush green olives. After floating in the Dead Sea we create
our own mud mask facials. My handsome friend organizes
his own belated bar mitzvah. After a day picking kiwis,
we gather in the kibbutz's basement bomb shelter. Katyusha
rockets are coming in tonight from southern Lebanon.

The skinniest white girl on the program tells me daily how fat
she is. We are roommates and I am twice
her size. The Mexican-American girl keeps being mistreated,
mistaken for Arab. She buys herself flowers
to distract. Mid-semester break we escape
to Cairo and Alexandria, to pyramids and beaches.

Back in Jerusalem, we stood vigil with the Women in Black,
meet gay activists, attend a Palestinian secret radical

meeting, location undisclosed—just show up here
and they will take you. Later that evening,
dinner with the Indian Jewish Women's Organization.

The next day, riding through Gaza, we get caught between
Palestinian children with rocks and Israeli tanks.
Crouched between bus seats we witness defiant
Palestinian women run toward Israeli tanks, anger
and stones their only weapons. Less than an hour later
we are lounging, drinking with the UN soldiers
at the Beach Club in Gaza. Rested up,
we happily return to Jerusalem. We had missed
our favorite falafel stand, the bakery with the best
challah bread and the Jerusalem dance club,
where the entryway sign read, *No Dogs & No Arabs.*

Morning, at the Lodge

It was not dark. It was not night. I was not
outside. I was not alone. I was not
with strangers. There were women
in the vicinity. A mother and two daughters
were preparing breakfast two rooms over
in the next hotel suite. We were all recovering
from your eldest daughter's extravagant wedding the night
before. Your niece, my friend, went outside
to make a telephone call. You came to say hello
in the fullness of daylight, sat too close on the couch
and put your gigantic arms around me
and your palm came down fully onto my breast.
Plain and clear. Plain as day. I jumped and ran
into another room. You went back
to your hotel suite. Your wife and daughters continued
to prepare breakfast. My friend came back and I told her
because we were in Madras and I had no one else
to tell. She said she cannot hear
of such things. Ten minutes later we all sat down together
for breakfast. You complimented the intricate design
on the sleeve of my dress. I sat wondering
whether you did this kind of thing to your own
daughters, or only to their best friends who came over to play.
Ten years later I still remember you. Today, at a museum exhibit
about Native American tipis. To simply appreciate
the beauty of the acquired, the beadwork of the colonized,
without any mention of the violations, of reparations,
is like sitting at breakfast in Madras. Trying to enjoy
that daughter's luminous newlywed smile, and that wife's
incredible, even when improvised, home-cooking.

Rolls Royce Quality Factory in China

The shoe distributor had his pitch down.
Our $400 women's pumps are only $200 now
since we moved production from Italy to our Rolls Royce
Quality Factory in China. The shoe consumer in me
battled with the workers' rights
advocate. My own pocketbook and desire
for fashion versus the sea and skies
and all of humanity. My own needs
for comfort and fashion, designed
by the foot surgeon turned shoemaker
warred with the likelihood that the lower the price
the closer the factory workers to a deathly
moment like the garment fire in Bangladesh
killing 112 people. Those workers produced goods
for Walmart after an earlier high-risk
violation. But the rule says
business would only be suspended
if there were three orange-level violations,
and so, onward. Besides, our Asian aunties need
their jobs. And we wouldn't want
any of these factories to close now, would we?

A Good Job for SK

My father gave me some good advice, she said,
as we sat chatting during our break
as we prepared for her testimony.

SK, with her head-covering
and beautiful daily-wear salwar kameez,
continued, *He told me
that if I study hard for my GED
and get into college and do well
then I can get a good job.
And in a good job, things like this
don't happen to girls.
Then, I can get a job where men don't
grab girls and try to kiss them
in the basements of 99 cents stores.*

Upon hearing this, my eyes fell
and my mind was unsure
whether or not to break this girl's delusion.
Whether to tell her that men grab
and kiss women in all kinds of "good jobs."
Women in million-dollar jobs
speak to me about presidents
of companies grabbing them, and worse.

I was unsure whether to explain
that some men in corporate positions
think they are even more powerful
than men who supervise six stores.
How to explain the complexities

of human resources policies
and how maybe in corporate jobs
they have pieces of paper
explaining sexual harassment,
but still, women report
men grabbing them and kissing them
no matter how much money some make
in their "good jobs."

I told her simply that, *Yeah, in some offices it is better
than other offices. And yeah, in some offices, it is better
than in these stores. And yeah, you should study hard
for your GED. And yeah, you should go to college.
And yeah, you should get a "good job."*

As we continued to prepare,
she gained confidence in sharing her story,
about how many times her manager said, *I love you*
and how many times he said, *You have to go out with me,
otherwise I could fire you.*

She had told him,
*You know we are both Muslims.
You know this is wrong
in our culture. Please stop
it, you know this is wrong.*

We went over how many times
he touched her shoulders and how many times
he grabbed her hands and how many times
he grabbed her waist in the basement, and how many times
he tried to kiss her. We continued to prepare
as she dreamed of a better job. And what I did not tell her
is I am so sorry, darling, to inform you
that your lovely, supportive father is wrong.

He is so wrong because studying hard
will not make the difference,
going to college will not save you,
and a "good job" cannot protect you
from these kinds of evil. From these evils,
which are often protected by the dead
silence in our communities. But not this time.

By the time this is over, these stores
will get their own pieces of paper
about sexual and other forms
of harassment, but only after paying a
monetary settlement to you.
And uncle manager man
will get some training, and some counseling.

And we survivors will carry forward
with our one small hope,
that this will be his last victim.
And that in any job, "good" or not,
more of us might be safe.

October 11, 2001

It kinda makes sense that I would be outside in 40-degree weather in a warm bubbly jacuzzi and feel at the same time these cold harsh winds and warm bubbly water. These are the kinds of extremes we are growing used to, these days of contrast. Hearing that our country has bombed a senior citizens' home in Afghanistan, and that our temporary office that replaced our 7 World Trade Center office finally got a fax machine, and that some people died of anthrax, all on the same day. Growing used to extremes. So many questions—is our country doing the right things? Taking away civil liberties is not the right thing. But they also say people are coming together more, reconciling, making things right, because we don't know if the end is near.

And now we know there are people who want to destroy us. Have you ever felt this afraid? For your country? Not as a female, not as a Black or brown person, but just as someone who lives in America? Is this how they feel in Palestine, picking olives and waiting for tanks, or for settlers with guns? Is this how they feel in Israel eating pizza and waiting for bombs to blow up? Is this how they feel in Kashmir, in Northern Ireland, in too many countries in South America, in Africa, in Asia, in Europe? Now, we are all afraid. Because anthrax does not see color and terrorist planes did not see class. Janitors were killed right there with the billionaires. Suicide bombers don't see immigration status or whether you believe in US foreign policy. Now we are all afraid.

And also afraid to wear Indian shawls when winter is coming. For six years I have worn my auntie's shawl. A kind of protest. Am I too afraid to protest? On the front door my roommate puts up a sign: *Honor their Memory with Peace.* Everyone else on the block has an American flag. I wonder if that is just making us a target for violence. I sound like a coward. And so I don't say out loud that siding with peace makes me feel afraid. Can I really wear a peace button to work when I work for the federal government?

My father in Illinois buys his first American flag decal for his automobile. His Sikh doctor friend shaves his hair. The Muslim girls down the block remove their head coverings. It is a shame. People are giving up being themselves, after all these years in America. This is a shame. People tell me this is New York, and so people should know the difference. The difference between Indian and Arab, but even some co-workers assume I speak Arabic. And then, the ignorant among the Indians say, *Hey, we are Indian, not Arab.* And the ignorant among the Hindus say, *Hey, we are Hindu, not Muslim.* As if it is now okay to look with suspect at some groups, some religions. Every religion has its fanatics. You know some Christians kill doctors who perform abortions. Is that in the name of your religion? You know some Jewish people kill Palestinians. Is that in the name of your religion? Some religious leaders bully gays in the name of their faith. Is that your faith leader?

None of this is in our names, or in the true name of any God. In most every group there are also believers in peace. Don't forget the Israeli soldiers who make known their views against the occupation. Don't forget the Catholics for Choice. Don't forget the Women in Black. Don't forget the LGBTQ Muslims. Don't forget. In every group, in every religious group, there are believers in peace. Honor their memory with peace.

The sticky remnants of packing tape Xs on Liyana's window

remind us that the dangers are not long behind. On our kitchen
windows remain too, these clear tape Xs, apparent only
in night-time skies. Super Storm Sandy, now weeks away,
though not gone for most of us. Buildings without power,
buildings that are no longer. From our routines lambasted,
to the man struck down, dead, by a tree while he slept
peacefully in his Queens apartment. A low-risk area. Nearby
our home, we see trees fallen throughout the streets
that could have come through our roof. Pema Chödrön
says the scientific evidence indicates we all fear
uncertainty, even more than physical pain.

For over 24 hours we had waited for the big storm
with a baby and a great-grandmother and the reality
of so little mobility between us. I packed one suitcase
with whatever was close at hand. Granola bars, coloring books,
and one change of clothes. An appointment for our first
professional family picture was not cancelled no matter
how many times I called to check. We smiled
and then put our fears aside long enough
to enjoy fish tacos on the Upper West
Side. The restaurant was going to close
at 4 p.m. so the workers could get home safely. At 3 p.m.
every table was filled with those of us who rely
on immigrant workers for our daily nourishment.

That afternoon, we found no water on the shelves,
no battery-powered radios left, and no gas
for the car. Bike riding as a family

was fun throughout the weekend,
but no longer come Monday morning.
The subways were still closed, and so I pushed the toddler
in the stroller for 45 minutes, so that we could vote
for President Obama. And now the radio declares
that the people approve of how the leaders handled
the crisis, while the public housing residents cry out
that FEMA did not come,
Bloomberg did not come,
and they still remain waiting.

Salvation Army

Volunteers travel to Breezy Point, New York,
and speak to the camera of Super Storm Sandy
and their *volunteer highs*. They bring canned food
and wool blankets to teary-eyed recipients, weary
with gratitude. My parents landed on the paradise
island of Jamaica in 1975. They had come to serve
with a church but, soon after arrival, one night
their Kingston hotel caught on fire. The missionaries
now themselves in need of some service. Left
on the streets in their nightclothes
with their three-year-old daughter. As an attempt to prove
her love, my mother once recounted: *Don't you get it,
I left my wedding sari, my gold jewelry, my valuables,
and took only you.* All I can remember
is sitting on the floor in some Kingston
family's living room with a teenage boy
who introduced me to his records and lent me
his headphones. Years later, my father's letter full
of the despair of job loss at age 55 still closed
with: *We made it through that Jamaica fire, we will
make it through this.* I think of my parents,
on their third day in Kingston,
and how the only time their daughter cried
was when she was forced to leave
that boy's living room, his headphones,
and all that good music.

The successful candidate should hail from a well-regarded law school

—Job posting, March 2013—

There are two schools of thought. You should go where you will feel the most comfortable, or you should go to a school that will open the most doors. *—1992, handwritten letter, in reply to mine, from Professor Patricia Williams*

In the weeks before the LSAT in 1993, I walked across
the college lawn, my only witness, the scent of freshly cut
grass. The library opened at eight and for one month,
every morning in the two hours before class, I studied
for this test that was the key to my future. Classmates complained
to my face, *You know you will get in to law school*
because you are a person of color. No relatives in this field, I knew
nothing of preparatory classes, no academic counselor
informed me of practice exams or asked to review my essay.
I used one study book purchased at a bookstore
over the summer. Every morning before classes I sat
in the library overlooking the snow-covered trees, trying
my hand at impossible logic puzzles and math games,
these building blocks of arguments. Improving my time,
slowly. Then, one morning, the mini-van to transport us
two hours away to the closest test in Bloomington,
Indiana, was late. Our tickets read, in bold print:

**NO ONE WILL BE ADMITTED
AFTER 8:30a.m.**

At 8:30 a.m. we sat completely still
at a red light on the outskirts of Bloomington. Upon arrival

the registration desk was left empty and on the third floor
of the campus building, we ran into a kind proctor
who had dipped into the hallway searching for his missing five
before beginning the exam. The five of us, breathless,
entered the room, filled in our names in little circles,
and began. And when I looked up, still breathless,
after entering my name, I still remember, the proctor smiled.

*And not long after, by 1996, California voters passed Prop 209,
a ban on affirmative action.*

My score reflected the less than ideal
circumstances of my testing. I forgot
to complete the easy puzzles first and then go back
to the difficult. It was the last test of the season. I ended up
where I belonged, a beloved public interest-focused law
school. One that my mother cannot find
at the top of most school-ranking charts
no matter how hard she looks
or how many times she asks me. When I had visited Harvard
Law School and sat on the bench outside the classroom,
another prospective student inquired: *So, when's your essay due
to your law school advisor?* But I knew of no such
person. The only person who read my essay
was my father. As for me, my reliance on grace
began to be well-practiced. And on some days, I am still,
waiting at that 8:30 a.m. red light. My chances
at well-regarded, simply dissipating before my eyes.

Refused to sign *(things I came across while reviewing 16 boxes of personnel files for my day job)*

—Dedicated to all the many workers who "refused to sign" when they are presented with discriminatory or retaliatory disciplinary notices. Supervisors often write "refused to sign" in place of the employees' signatures at the bottom.

Friendly, dynamic, a go-getter!
It continues to be my pleasure to supervise and work with her.

Commendable flexibility. A cheerful willingness.

Performs with growing confidence and efficiency.

Provides exemplary care to residents.

We love Madeline.

Reliable, empathetic.

Reliable, flexible, conscientious.

You come in and do your work, quietly and competently.
Having said that, there are several issues to address.

She needs to be more judicious in her use of sick time.

Atta boy letters.

Wonderful, a lot of personality.

Kind and competent.

The foresight to know what needs to be done, without being asked.

She will question something that doesn't seem right or is unfair but does not argue with those in authority just to argue. She is easy to work with but one cannot take advantage of her. She gets along with others but has a mind of her own and strong opinions.

Flexible, caring, efficient.

Improvements: Attendance, Communication,
& Remember to smile.

Customer service should be performed with more effort, vigor, and a smile.

Three hospital housekeepers were written up
for an unauthorized ice cream break.

Obsessive, in a good way. Will be an asset to us.

Ensures that the document that is scanned is legible.

I write to advise you we have received a wage garnishment.

To find a job where I can be rewarded
and challenged at the same time.

Pleasant demeanor.

Wants to grow.

All Rise

Hey, thanks for being nice—what the Whole Foods grocery delivery guy said to my friend, Pia.

When the back of the house kitchen staff at Ollie's pulls up a seat in the front, at 89th and Broadway in Manhattan and starts snipping off the ends of 10,000 green beans in my exact line of vision, why do I feel less at ease sipping hot and sour soup on a winter's day? Somehow my conscience feels better when your work remains invisible, when there is a wall, sheetrock between us.

In my Brooklyn elevator when the nanny asks, *Which family in the building do you work for?* I feel shame, pride, and solidarity as I grip my daughter's hand tight. Is it because I recognize you? Is it my brown skin? Is it my smile? Something felt recognized. Amma's family home has rubber trees on three sides, but alas, inheritance passes through the sons, despite Mary Roy's court case. In the Ohio village I watched her make all of the kape, all of the chai. She would take a small spoonful of each cup to check it for enough sweetness before delivering the tray to the church visitors, alongside plantain chips and biscuits.

Age 10, visiting my aunts' Kerala kitchens, I always wanted to take a turn, sitting on the floor with the coconut scraper. *Scrape, scrape, scrape.* Leaving much too much coconut meat in the shell but they still gave me that, *Good job for an American Girl* smile. But after the first 10 scrapes, the work turned to pure drudgery. I moved on to the mortar and pestle *pound, pound, pounding* the spices but soon left it behind, to lay on the bed and read every single one of the *Reader's Digests* in their glass cabinets. By evening the green bean thoren was ready for us. Auntie would say, *Look, Sunu, this was your work, do you see your coconut there in the dish?* The next day, in the Kerala village, I watched Ammachi use the fibers from baby coconuts to keep the fire going. She even killed one of their chickens from the backyard for the special occasion of the last supper of our visit.

Years later, during the middle of law school, I learned this rule by observation: we must stand when the judge enters the courtroom. One afternoon, I watched the law clerk run back to her desk from the law library to put on her suit jacket when called, before going to Judge Houston's chambers. In that moment I learned much of what I needed to know about the law. The founder of my family's faith, Quakerism, was jailed for not bowing before the king. And here I am, standing up, every time a judge enters the courtroom. Pound, pound, on the door. *All rise. You may be seated. Good afternoon, counsel. Good afternoon, Your Honor.* These practices we've accepted as commonplace, as commoners. During many settlement negotiations in back chambers, I sit on the couch with the federal judge. The judge is wearing her black robe, and I have kept on my grey suit jacket for the entire afternoon.

And now I still witness, in a Zoom court hearing, another judge said the white male government lawyer's name at least 10 times, and said the young South Asian woman lawyer's name, zero times.

Back at my office in Manhattan, I give the new cleaning lady various gifts in exchange for taking the garbage. First an apple, then an orange, then two pairs of gently used dress shoes. After our chats, she takes them all, but we never learned each other's names.

And the time we left Delhi, to take the toddler to Kerala, we took all our remaining rupees into Rohini's mother's kitchen. How else to say thank you for all the meals they brought to us, literally on a cart, rolled into our room. The new toddler sleeping soundly on the floor. They brought chapathis, dal, rice, thoren, curries, and pickles. We left them with only a small sequined blue silk purse from Fabindia. We had placed inside whatever rupees we had left on-hand. We did not speak the same language, and I cannot remember if we tried to determine their names. We did not ask the madam of the house permission to go into her kitchen. The youngest cook, she was wearing red rubber chappels, and I was wearing navy blue tennis shoes.

Back in the States, when my cousin and her new husband cut into their wedding cake, when they put both their hands on the knife and looked up and smiled, they had their backs to me. I witnessed one of the women catering staff take the groom's hand and put it so swiftly around my cousin's waist. I do not know this woman's name who worked at the most light-filled wedding venue in downtown Madison. I do believe that it is because of her that the photograph on the front of their wedding thank you card that came in the mail appeared just so flawless.

And now, at 4501, we smile and say hello at least two times a day. Your pandemic mopping went from once to twice to three times daily. I can tell you if there's water pooled by the second-floor stairs. I can laugh with you when we overhear your co-workers joking around. And then one day I broke through the wall of shyness, or perhaps, snobbery, and I just asked. I learned that your name is Reina, meaning queen.

Onam in Manhattan

Far away from Kerala
banana trees that gave us these
once-frozen banana leaves
to use as our plates,
we sit and recreate tradition
of what they do in the place
we call *Back Home*.

Sitting on the floor
with our cream-colored clothes,
hungry eyes, we are served
rice and coconut curries, countless
vegetable dishes and
spicy pickles on the side.

Side by side we are happily
eating away with our hands,
everyone quiet and busy, when she asks,
You eating your mango pickle?
Yes, of course, I reply,
but still allow her to share some of mine.

She reaches over with
her curry-stained-rice-bits-dripping hand.
She leans in close and
takes more than half of my mango pickle
from my shiny green banana leaf plate.

Now we are bonded, I say
as I sat there wanting to believe

that she felt some special affection
for me, if she'd take my mango pickle so freely
on the same day that we had met.

But I already could tell
that this was the kind of girl
who would take mango pickle so freely
from almost anyone's banana leaf.

Diverted

Walking by he grabbed my arm,
kind but insistent, and handed me
a small piece of yellow gold
soap and spoke to me of the Dead
Sea. Hoping to divert, I said, *I've lived*
in Jerusalem. I've bathed in the Dead
Sea before. He again grabbed
my arm and led me to the sink
with water at the back of the booth
at the Grand Central Station Holiday
Bazaar. *So then you know, come in*
and try our new scrubs. For my final group
project in Jerusalem we had studied water
rights in Israel/Palestine and how water was made
as divided as everything else. Meaning, the children
in the refugee camps had very little.
Meaning the tourists in Haifa were fine,
and we students at the Gloria
Hotel in the Old City of Jerusalem enjoyed plenty
with our morning toast and jam. The kiwi plants
at the kibbutz, next to the children's yoga
class, never went without
water. But the refugee camps,
they featured zero swimming pools.

Carpe Diem Kombucha

Options galore we sat at Kripalu
and considered our Saturday
afternoon. Debating the sauna or the whirl-
pool or a medium-long hike. We contemplated
browsing in the bookstore, laying down
for a nap, or walking to see the pond
at the far end of the yoga center. We debated
café offerings of kombucha, green tea or pineapple
juice. The choices so many and so pleasant that we just sat
tilting our heads, ears almost touching our shoulders
on one side, and then the other. *We could do this,*
or we could do that…. But nothing brought us to the present
like D. arriving to join our table. She knew what she wanted.
She wanted to try cranberry kombucha. A decision
was made. We pooled our dollars and gathered
four paper cups. When we cheered,
the cups clinked with the same import as the finest
wine glasses. When D. arrived,
it all crystallized. The group would try
cranberry kombucha. Earlier that morning,
we had learned about how D. chatted up Maya
once upon a time while students sat painting
on a campus. And when we finally drank it,
the taste of kombucha was as alarming
and peaceful as D.'s voice that morning.
She had shared with the group
her recent diagnosis. She had only been given
a few months to live.

Sexism

Lovely restaurant basement
holiday lunch with colleagues. Federal government
workers pay for ourselves—pasta, salmon, chocolate
cake. I stare down my 10-year certificate and pin
my hopes on some other future. Civil
rights advocacy and pensions delightful but still.

Former director walks by and says to sole male
attorney sitting with us three (not once, but twice):
You got yourself three pretty
ladies there with you. You got
three whole ladies to yourself.
How is it guy talk if we are right
here, smart and invisible. The first time quiet
the second I say to the new male colleague, laughing,
Just leave it to him to be consistently
inappropriate. Sports talk to begin every staff
meeting is one thing, but seeing three lady
senior trial attorneys as only ladies, as only
accessories, another altogether. Even I can laugh
at holiday jokes, but then later just check
who gets promoted.

Laughing while cringing among smart,
sexist, once-handsome men, is in all females'
job descriptions. If you are lucky,
that is the extent of it.

Trueing

The hammock breaks like clockwork
and the months drizzle on
with faint fireworks. Regrouping the clothesline
she climbs in again, humming a tune.
This uncomfortable backseat
too breezy, this slim torso so strange, she's addicted
to the way food is shared,
the way the rug pulls out, but not
quite. The brain's only resting
place, this reckless mystery.

Teenage girls sexually harassed
in the back of suburban stores,
Rastafarian security guards disciplined
for keeping dreadlocks,
Long Island policemen transferred out
to worse positions, in the name of
their advancing age, South Asian waiters
harassed, called *Taliban* at the Plaza Hotel,
on a daily basis after 9/11. A parade
of my traumatized, but determined,
partners ride by, leaving all of us
changed for the good, and grateful.

Yet, every Sunday morning,
the pastor's kid still wakes up
seeking. Waiting for the water to boil
in the morning, and the mustard seeds
to sound in the evening.

Too Pretty

October on the subway, roses at my side,
kids being loud. One skinny girl
with a cap and a pretty smile
gets up to give me her seat
and takes this chance to sit
on her friend's lap. I read the paper
and look over at these girls. So free
and easy, they are laughing laughing.
I look at the pink pink roses
and how I say I am not a romantic
and how this whole roses thing
is going to ruin my reputation
against romance. I watch the girls. I watch
the skinny girl in boy's clothes and pretty smile
flirt with all the other girls. So free
and easy, they are laughing laughing.

And the man next to me, he is also watching watching.
And the man next to me, he leans over and says to me:

Hey, miss, hey miss, that's too pretty to be a boy, right?

As if somehow that thought disgusts him.
As if he wants some agreement about this disgust.
And me, I am just relieved that he knows
that I am a miss and not a pretty boy. So I just shrug,
and I say nothing because I am still
afraid. Afraid to say what does a she look like
and what does a boy look like. And what does too pretty
look like and what is your problem exactly. And I don't know

whether his disgust is that he thinks girls who look
like boys should be beat
up or boys who look like girls should be beat
up because, in fact, we know, they both are. I only know
that I was relieved that he did not know my pink
pink roses were for a girl and somehow I have this safety
of passing. And I think to myself:
You all sitting there, laughing laughing
sitting there on your sixth grade girlfriend's lap,
so free and easy, laughing laughing,
be safe my handsome girls, be safe my pretty boys.

TWO

One of Us

Sleet

*Sleet occurs when snowflakes falling through a small layer of warm air in
the atmosphere begin to melt. The melting snowflakes then refreeze when
they pass into a layer of colder, freezing air.*

The weatherman said, *Sleet is usually a transition
moment in the weather. It just holds the place
between snow and rain.* But today, the sleet
has lasted all day long. I walk home
in the Friday evening sleet, painful
and unrelenting. There was nothing
transitional about it.

And this is how it feels,
with my family.

Stuck in this land between
acceptance and rejection,
a moment that should have been transitional,
but instead, several years of sleet. Not disowning me
but not quite allowing me in, either.

One day everyone is warm
and laughing, and the next it's as if
five separate conversations never
took place. The conversations become so slippery
that sometimes I must stop
calling altogether. Until the next pretty
and deceptive email, *look, we won
marriage.* My father tells others
that he has no Biblical, or theological issue,
with his daughter being gay. It's just he wished

that she was married to a man
and had a couple of kids.

One day it's the lovely snowflake
of *how is she doing,* and even singing songs
at our wedding. And the next it's the painful
hailstorm of no pictures on their mantel.

And yet, how can I possibly leave them
for good, when I am still thrown

something so promising,
every 11th conversation.

Comrades

The perfectly lovely landlord emails us about broken backyard lights, problematic doorknobs, and the yearly rent increase. He starts each email with, *Dear comrades*. It always makes me giggle—like we are part of some secret Marxist revolutionary group, which we should be, but we are not. The truth of the matter is we didn't even make it to the last anti-war rally.

These days, when I think of comrades, I think of the other women at the infertility clinic. Before she takes my morning blood the nurse asks for my DOB. As she types it in, a good 23 names pop up on the computer screen, at just one such clinic.

The nurse calls for the other South Asian lady in the waiting room, Shivaani. The nurse calls for the Orthodox Jewish lady with her long skirts and black patent leather flats, and then she calls for the Black woman who always comes alone and sits and knits. She calls the Latina woman in her track suit and fancy sneakers. She calls the white woman who drives in from Westchester with her gigantic diamond rings. She calls the one who is late for work, the one who does not have to work, the one whose insurance covers this, the one whose parents gave her the money, the one who put this all on her credit cards, and the one who pays $10,000 per cycle out of pocket. The nurse calls the stylish lady with her Prada purse, the hipster chick with the cool haircut, the business ladies with their blackberries, and the other dykes who smile at us. The nurse calls the embarrassed couple here for their first visit.

The rest of us started that way, but we have now sat here for so long that we've almost forgotten to feel ashamed.

We all sit and wait for our follicles to mature, for our eggs to appear and for them to be taken out and fertilized. As then we wait for the embryos to be placed inside of us and to implant properly.

The 28-year-old Indian nurse asks if I am giving myself the injections or if my partner is giving me the injections. When I respond saying my partner, she says to me smiling, *He'll get used to it - he is going to be a pro in no time.* It's as if she only made it to half the sensitivity training session since she learned to use the word partner but still missed out on all the many reasons why. Or maybe she knows, but thought for sure this would not apply to her South Asian patients.

We light a candle before we listen to the doctor's Christmas Eve voicemail message: *Both eggs have fertilized. Come in on Tuesday at 11 a.m. for the embryo implantation.*

The nicest of all the doctors says as he inserts the two embryos, *Say goodnight to your babies.* It is one day after Christmas and the Jewish doctor says to me, *What's one more miracle, in this Christmas season.*

The same night that I got my second positive pregnancy test results my parents sat in Chicago, not knowing any of this, and told themselves they would never become grandparents. They called the next morning and asked if I was still planning to adopt as I had mentioned some years ago. I told them that I was pregnant.

Walking in Battery Park to avoid going into my office while crying I realized I had to inform them that the pregnancy did not last. Their only response, *Life does not always work out as we plan.* They manage to take a sympathetic tone as they quickly changed the subject.

At my 34th birthday party two separate friends inquired about the children I promised them five years ago. *What's up, dude? Weren't you supposed to have kids, like five years ago? Hell-O-o?! What happened, dude, the clock is ticking. You need to get on it!* I mumble something about how sometimes things just take longer than you think.

Yes, I tried acupuncture. Yes, I took my waking temperature. Yep, checked my cervical mucus. Yes, I saw that doctor. I know, I am only 34. Yes, I know the 50-year-olds are having babies. Of course, I know I could certainly adopt.

I try my best to comfort my friends' anxieties.

And while I sat waiting for just one of my seven embryos to properly implant: Maya was born and then Jose, and then Diego, and then Alejandro; then Saira and Zarif; then Hussayn and Joe and Gabriel; followed by Benjamin and Cole and Elias and Evan; and Elana and Mia and Solana and another Mia; then Hannah was born and then Emelia—with an E and Caleb came along; then Taryn aka TJ and Oscar; and Onamika in Boston, then Zade in San Francisco and Adeline and Sammy in Chicago, Jyoti in Denver and then Eloisa was born in Boston, and Karishma was born in Philadelphia and then Liyana and Sahil and Priya and Sumathi. These stunning babies with their perfect names all arrived to greet the world.

And then my friends each began to have their second child. And that just seemed to be the height of unfairness. Like my dearest single friend asks me, *Why do you get to go on flirty coffee dates when you are practically married? Shouldn't everyone have one cake before some people get to have two? Shouldn't everyone have one home before some people get to have two?* But whether it's cakes, or homes, or coffee dates, or babies, this is just not how the world operates as it relates to the things we desire most.

I decide not to keep paying out-of-pocket for the special infertility-issues therapist who tells me, *This must be really hard for you.* Yet, in my one visit she reassures me: *It's 100% normal to want to rip up holiday cards with pictures of your friends' smiling babies.*

And when a comrade becomes pregnant, there was an extra and intense joy. And then I would feel even more alone. Like we are not comrades any longer. It's like in the old days when one's queer friends entered heterosexual marriages. One is happy they found love, and one also felt more alone and without the company you once kept. It's not judgmental, it's a feeling.

And then, the people who never wanted kids in the first place and used to tell me that, often and loudly, those people—those people, they began to have babies.

And also, daily, I think about all the many children in the world without any parents at all. And I feel guilty, but not any better. I know that seven failed embryos warrant at least one full night of tears. And yet I also know there are 70 times seven children waiting for parents to love them.

I cannot forget the people dying in wars, soldiers and so many civilians, or any of the world's more worthwhile tragedies. The poem feels self-indulgent and necessary, as I do not pretend, even for one minute, that this is the worst tragedy I have heard about this year, or even this month. But it is, most certainly, mine.

Grade Four Peaches

The Board Certified Specialist Doctor gave me these parting words: *Do what your Grandmother's Ghost tells you to do.* He told me this when I insisted on some additional, perhaps magic, instructions that would make it all work out this time. I left the appointment with two fertilized embryos inside me. The Board Certified Specialist Doctor said I had produced grade-four eggs. When I asked what this meant he said, *Imagine we are talking about peaches and that you are sorting them into categories. The best ones are rated grade five—those would go to a restaurant—now we never see grade five but grade-four eggs are very good, they are like the grade of peaches that would go out in front on the fruit display stand.* Earlier the embryologist had also said that these were *beautiful* embryos. She did not come off as someone who would go around casually handing out compliments, and so I decided to believe her.

The Board Certified Specialist Doctor—trained in giving patients in just my situation, Only Realistic Expectations— said as he completed the procedure: *Say goodnight to your babies.* He was smart enough to know that somehow we can train ourselves to hold hope, love, and realistic expectations in our hearts at the same time. He told me to be brave, and he was not talking about the many painful injections, in my hip and in my stomach, or the many bitter medicines, but to be brave, instead, with my heart. I took another deep breath and wished for the good cells to multiply.

I decided to follow the Board Certified Specialist Doctor's instructions—this doctor who talked about working in his garden and who had his daughter playing the piano as his cell phone's ring tone. This doctor who invited my partner into the room on his own initiative for the medical procedures. So based on his warm personality and his medical credentials, I decided to follow his last bit of medical advice: To do what my Grandmother's Ghost tells me to do.

The Grandmother's Ghost is my father's mother. She has been a ghost for 17 years, for the second half of my life. The clearest memory I have of her is that she cried and cried with happiness whenever we would arrive to visit her in a place called Vengal outside of the village of Thiruvalla in Kerala, India. This scene took place about once every four years during my childhood. I was terrified by the depth of her love and by how long she would cling to my father upon his arrival. My parents did not tell her the precise dates of our trips so that in case there were delays she would not worry. So she was given some hint that we might come during a particular month and then we would just arrive. Grandmother waited and waited for my father's visits and cried with joy when he came home and cried with sadness when he left, and again, began her long wait.

My Grandmother's Ghost teaches me patience. She tells me to love, even though these beings may not come to me for a long time, and even though I have no idea if, or when, they will ever come to me. She tells me to love even if these beings are just an idea, even if I have to imagine them. She tells me to love, as the beings may arrive as an adopted child, five years from now. She tells me to love the idea of them, and to know that it is only love that can hold the magnitude of the efforts that went into my family's creation. From my Grandmother's Ghost I learn that sometimes you have to wait a long time for beings you love and sometimes you are quite sad while you are waiting. I learned from her that tears can be complicated and can mean a lot of things at once. Like I am so glad that you are finally here, and that I am mad that it took so long. I learned from my Grandmother's Ghost that love is to be expressed, that hugs can be long, and that you should allow your children to pursue their dreams, even in distant lands. I learned from her, that you may not know how and when your children will come to you.

Rebuilding Efforts

I wore a black kurta shirt. With blue
jeans and black boots. I wore no
jewelry. It was the first time I had ventured
into social after all that
solitude. I had wanted to talk,
to no one. Just wanted to sit by Shalini,
and so I sat and breathed
in, three times, for each in-breath. The dancers
fused the Modern with the Classical Indian, and
I was distracted by a few moments of color,
movement, after so much sitting
at home. I avoided speaking to everyone
but the lead dancer's mother, visiting
from Arizona. Is this how the first outing felt
for you? The first after
a death, job-loss, break-up, or your own
specific kind of despair? When did NYC begin
again, after 9/11? Do you remember
what you wore on that night?

International adoption agencies maintain strict rules for the maximum individual and combined ages of parent-applicants

When she turns 20 and I am 57

will I help her decorate her dorm room and
will I bite my tongue every time I want to start
with, *Sweetie, why you didn't call me last weekend?*

When she turns 15 and I am 52

will we one day sit on the metro
in a foreign city and will she hold
the map, all by herself, studying the routes? Will I fan
myself cursing menopause and will we carry five
shopping bags already between us?

When she turns 10 and I am 48

will she play soccer, and if her team loses will I hug her
with the same tightness as when they win?

When she turned one and I turned 38

did she know she would be celebrating her next
birthday in Brooklyn with a whole cupcake
from the Chocolate Room, instead of at the children's home
in South India, and did I?

When she was born and I was 37

did she know that in three years someone would yell to us
across the NYC subway car, *Hey, was she a premmie?*
and that I would have no answer at all
to such a question, no answer at all?

Provenance Unknown

(phrase used by the Brooklyn Museum to designate paintings from "unknown" origins)

In the full elevator this morning a co-worker asks:

So, what's going on with the news?
You had said something about maybe by June.

I do not know what you accomplished today. I do not know
if you have allergies. I do not know
how many biscuits you ate today. I do not know
if the other adoptive parents took videos
where you may appear in the background.
I do not know if you turned your face to the camera
now as you did in the picture
when you were three-months-old. I do not know
if the caretakers are still giving you two biscuits
or one or none. I do not know
if CARA will approve. I do not know
if the court will approve. I do not know
if the courts will be backlogged
after their May recess. I do not know
which judge will get my submissions. I do not know
if everything will work out. I do not know.

I do not know.
I do not know.

No, I do not know yet, about June.

Knowledge

In the newest photograph from the orphanage
I can tell you had been crying
by the remnants

of snot, clear, slight snot coming down
from your nose. And now I know
how Mom knew about those nights

that I was off to conduct great
mischief. She knew I signed
Dad's name, that one time I got a D

on a math test. She knew that when I was five, I broke
my school friend's watch. She understood in her heart
that junior prom was not something to be missed,
in this land. And now, I can already tell

at least 40 things about you, my baby,
just from one new photo. You
had been crying, real

tears. As the investigators are taught,
it's only real if the nose starts
to run. You had been crying

and then someone came to snap
a photo because some lady
in the States kept seeking

an update. So the last in the chain
went and witnessed you, and put on for you a blue
doggy dress, falling off your one-year-old frame
and you kept crying. And then she gave you
one biscuit and then you kept crying

and then she gave you two. Good
for you for making them give you two before
you would stop. You already know this much

about negotiations and hungers. And of this fact
I am proud, as much as it breaks me daily.

Kasthaputta Vanhu

(But they came all the way here already, taking such troubles.)

When we left the Indian orphanage
last August, we left our baby

formula, sweets, diapers, lotion, lice
shampoo and even the travel umbrella
from my chosen sister's handbag. We took in return

only an image of her, rocking
herself, and a traced outline of her left
foot. The floral pattern on my light green
notebook could not hide 10 years
of dismay, but now it contained one footstep

towards something possible. My narrow
notebook like the ones made of scraps
from the printing press given for free
to the workers. That season
Mary Oliver worked at the press she said
she wrote only narrow poems.

We had arrived with one pair
of toddler shoes, brown,
size seven, with pink flowers, but much
too large for her tiny feet. I now carried

an accurate drawing of her left
foot throughout Brooklyn, searching
for something small and perfect enough,
that could be revered later in remembrance
as her first pair of shoes from me.

Now, one year later, a little girl
in brown and pink shoes skips
down the subway corridor
holding my hand on her morning
commute from Fort Greene
to her preschool in Lower Manhattan.

First Trip to Underhill Park

I.

The nice lady at MOMA had said earlier that morning, *it's so funny, her hair is so straight and your hair is so curly*. I responded, curtly, *yes, well, she's adopted*. You only had 30 minutes of your 90-minute nap on that day. You had recognized the letter S for the first time. You tried ice cream for the first time on that day. It was a painful experience—like when the nice doggies get too close. You loved the taste of the coconut ice cream but it was too much coldness. You kept going in for a bite and then you couldn't stand the cold, but you wanted this sweetness so much. You stood on Underhill Avenue and cried real tears at this quandary. Is that how adoption feels to us? When you saw two Indian girls playing at the park your eyes followed their every move. I imagined you might be thinking back of the girls from the school next door to the orphanage who would come and visit every afternoon. You stared at them until we left. Although your mouth moved, no words came out.

II.

You cried all the way home that day, even when
I carried you. When you came in the door
you didn't say wow as was your practice.
You only kept crying. We sat in the hallway right inside
the door, with the door closed so that I could cry
too. I hugged you and you were eventually distracted
by the sequins on my gray shirt—and took solace
in the routine of hanging up your scarf
on the hook all by yourself. After taking off your socks
and shoes you accidentally placed two socks in one

of your silver and yellow tennis shoes and then
wondered how one of the socks went so suddenly
missing. I pointed and showed you how
two socks were mistakenly stuck together
in one shoe. You took the two out,
carefully separated one from the other, and
placed each one where it belonged.

For it has been observed that it takes 20 minutes for your belly to tell your brain, *I am full*

I have come to understand my toddler daughter
swallows her lunch whole. Preschool teacher informs
the babysitter, and she informs us. We are told
other children stare, watch as she inhales
everything, in one breath. No meal ever enough, always
asks for seconds. Teacher helps make sure one thing is left
unopened in the lunchbox so she will have something left,
when it's time for afternoon snack. Like her grandfather,
and her mother, our toddler eats quickly and tracks whether
there is more. A lifetime of hearing Mom demand
Slow down. Eat slowly. Some unquenchable fire, some unfulfilled
craving. And, perhaps, our origins are even closer
than we could have imagined. As one aunt proclaimed,
albeit tenderly, upon their first meeting, *Wow, she looks like,*
she looks like, she could be, one of us.

Fake Help Opening the Fake Ketchup

Despite efforts spent promoting equal time for trucks,
dolls, tractors and tutus, she now always reaches
for the play kitchen and dishes. Serves us pretend broccoli,
rice, fish, and ice cream. When she brings out the fake
hot dogs, she insists that we help open
the ketchup. It won't open, we explain, showing her
how the plastic lid is fused permanently
to the bottle. She looks baffled, wondering how we
could be so confused, since everyone knows:
one fake helps, to fake open, the fake ketchup.

Pausing an Argument to Attend Our First Parent-Teacher Conference on Valentine's Day

This must be the same blank stare that some divorced parents
possess while riding the elevator to meet with teachers. Security
guards must view us in these cameras, face forward,
feet locked in each corner. Stuck wishing for more space
for our own elevator cars, buildings, neighborhoods, and cities.
All the parents make the same joke: *Did your baby pass?*
Teachers say our toddler *listens, doesn't fuss, plays well,*
and shares. But, yes, she is behind in some ways compared
to her classmates (stated in this way only
because I asked such a question). I am reassured again
and again, *it's an advanced group of three-year-olds. Most were born*
here, into this program, a couple of years before your daughter arrived
to this country. Most have older siblings, so just know, it's an advanced
group of threes. We are shown how she was asked to cut out
half a heart and she simply made snips all along the edges
of the pink construction paper. She was asked to write
her name and she made a large scribble on the page.
She only mixed up the V and the Y when tested
on the alphabet, but she somehow forgot
the all-important S. As for the numbers, she called
the six a nine, but also correctly called the nine a nine.
She knew most all her colors, only mistakenly
referring to black as brown. Still she also knew that
brown was brown. They suggested: *Her writing can improve*
with trying to write. Her fine motor skills could be improved
with small tasks that use her fingers. And so, that night
I asked her to try to uncap the toddler toothpaste,
all by herself, for the first time. We played with the toy

rotary phone for the first time since her arrival,
one year before. The co-parent had taken careful notes
of all of the teachers' finer points. But I only memorized
them, watching each word engrave
into the concrete of my slowly thawing heart.

Picking up Linzer Torte Cookies for the Quaker Potluck

Mom would come home from every church
reception with one cookie, wrapped in a napkin,
in her purse, only for me. Last night, for the first time,
I tried this trick too. It's not that we couldn't stop
and buy you an entire box of cookies, on any given day. It's that
we don't. And in 30 years you may imagine me
standing among the grown-ups and the chatter
of super storms, job losses and preschools, thinking
instead for a moment of you. You and the dance you would do,
when handed one shortbread cookie with a cut-out heart
of shining red raspberry jam. You and the dance
you would do, hands in the air, hips swaying, *Thank you, Amma,*
Thank you, Amma, as you bit into the delight
of one childhood Tuesday evening. Stopping, only to search
my face, to decipher, whether I came home with anything more.

Twenty Years of Coats

—Title from a conversation with my friend, Pia Deas. Sending a grateful shout-out to all the friends who gave us bags of kids' clothes and to the ones who later took our such bags. And shout-out also to Lulu's in Brooklyn and to ThredUp for all the gently used clothes and for helping us to save our money and the planet.

Light blue coat from Angela much too baggy, pink
coat from Mira, still stained after two trips
to the laundromat. It is the first cold day,
and I fumble and dress my toddler in make-do brown
fleece and pink butterfly

vest. Kneeling at her preschool cubby, I see
for the first time her cubbymate's winter coat. Storybook
gray purple wool with light gray lining and silver intricately
designed buttons. All my years of brown immigrant

longing stirred: wishes first for Nikes, then Izods, then new cars
on 16th birthdays. And now the desires simply
shift to commute-friendly renovated homes

in Park Slope, or three-bedroom homes by the promenade
in Brooklyn Heights. Crouched inches from that refined
wool, I loudly unzip my kid's bright pink vest, say nothing
but my gaze shifts again to this other kid's coat. Relieved
when I notice a bit of fraying

on the edge of one of the sleeves. Never cared
about any other Manhattan mother's Gucci purse
or Jimmy Choo high heels, but this time I walk away

that morning and purchase a new coat. Size three, stainless and fitted at the waist, in knee-length navy blue, as my longings face the latest cold day, of a never-ending season.

Teaching My Daughter To Re-Cap the Toddler Toothpaste

Don't push hard, don't push hard, don't push

so hard, no need to press

it so. Just place it gently on top, let it settle

into its place, and only then, gently

twist. Not that way, not that way,

the other way. Try one way,

try one way, and if it doesn't work, then stop,

then stop, then stop completely,

and then, try another way. Trust me,

trust me, you will know,

when it is time to stop turning.

To Satya, From Satya

Before I left home for the last day of the writers' conference, I placed the blank cards, the heart stickers, the 18 envelopes and the list of first grade kids' names on the dining table. We made a sample card early in the morning, even before my daughter ate her cereal. We went through each step: fold the paper in half, place the large felt heart sticker on the cover, write *Happy Valentine's Day* and *Love, Satya* on the inside, and then write the classmate's name on the envelope. I passed along these instructions to the babysitter, and trusted that she would pass the assignment supervision baton on to my spouse who would arrive in a couple hours after a week away for work. One way or another, between all of us, these 18 cards would be completed by the end of the weekend.

This was our fifth Valentine's Day together since our daughter joined the family at age almost two. Making cards was always fun at first, or for the first five even, but once a kiddo is writing her name for the sixth time, with 12 more looming ahead, it can be overwhelming. A better mom would have purchased supplies weeks in advance so that the work could be spread among several weekends but after becoming a parent I was finding it harder and harder to meet any deadlines with time to spare. This year I assigned the task to all of us for the weekend before Valentine's Day.

It wasn't until I was seven did I experience my first Valentine's Day. I was born in the United States and our family moved to Port Antonio, Jamaica, when I was three and returned when I was seven. One day at school, in the cold of February, soon after our return to the States, we each made decorated paper bags and I wasn't sure what the bags were for until that afternoon. At some point, the students all distributed small cards into these bags, and I must have sat there looking confused or just trying to act normal. The thing I do remember is that the teacher asked us each to pick a favorite card and then we went around the room and read that card aloud. The most memorable part of the afternoon was that the teacher said that all the cards she received were her favorite, and she read every single one aloud. I remember thinking she was a good teacher because she wanted each student to feel special. I also remember going home and putting one of these cards (I must have erased the name on it and put mine instead) in my parents' mailbox outside our apartment that evening. My immigrant parents must have found it so strange to see a small envelope, the size of their palm, with a card containing red and pink hearts from their seven-year-old.

And now, over 30 years later, I was in their shoes. When I arrived home that night after the conference, full up with Rita Dove's witty piece on prose poetry, Terrance Haynes and all his poems with the same title, Ocean Vuong's poems about his mother, poems from Ross Gay about his fig plants, and Aracelis Girmay's accountings of a Black boy looking at the stars, I saw one lone card sitting on the table. From the other room I tried to read it—I expected it would be for me, perhaps, or for a visiting auntie, or for my spouse. Upon closer inspection, the card said: *To Satya, From Satya*. I thought to myself, she must have gone through the names, and then wrote her own without realizing that she could avoid this arduous task for her own name. However, I later learned from my spouse that our child purposefully made herself this card. She had declared that she did not want to feel left out. After all, she had asked, why shouldn't she also have a card that's folded in half, with a felt heart sticker, and with a *Happy Valentine's Day* message inside, just for her.

Impulse Buys

On the drive home from a week-long family meditation camp, the next available bathroom break for our nine-year-old daughter was at an in-door, out-door Pennsylvania flea market.

Inside the market, we were drawn to all manner of colorful knickknacks, handmade soaps, and so many kinds of toys. After using the facilities, the kiddo asked if we could peruse a few of these booths. Recalling my week of training on mindful, be-in-the-moment parenting, and to my child's surprise, I agreed. After we smelled the lavender soap, the lemon soap, and the peppermint soap, she spotted a booth with thousands of shiny rocks and pebbles. This kid had a daily habit of selecting five small stones from the schoolyard and asking if she could bring them all home. When I limited this to one, she would reluctantly land on just one to bring home each day—carefully studying each one's crystals, stripes, and colors before deciding on the one.

At the shiny stones and rocks booth, I am unusually patient. I even consider spending a few dollars on a few pebbles. She seemed to sense that, without me saying a word, and I could feel her heart smile.

And then in one instant, everything changed. Looking toward the cashier, she saw, just hanging out there on the wall, real guns in real life.

Even after all the school lockdown drills of, *We will give you candy if you stay in the closet together and be real quiet,* and all the TV news of schools shootings, she had yet to witness real guns in real life.

She immediately dropped the pebbles and pleaded, *Amma, let's go. Please, Amma, let's get back in the car right now.*

My spouse and her car keys were somewhere in the area but not easily found, and so we quickly walked toward the furthest end of the parking lot. All the while, the kiddo looked back at this building that contained the fragrant homemade soaps, the toys, the shiny stones, and the guns.

This child, who knows I don't even approve of water guns. This child, who reports back to me, nervously, after she plays even marginally violent video games at friends' homes, appeared shocked at my seeming nonchalance.

I tried to form the right mindful, loving parent words to say everything was okay, that we were okay.

Yet, I was so half-hearted in my reassurance, that we just kept moving away, as far away as we could. For, in the end, I just wasn't sure, if her level of terror was more accurate than mine.

Distance Learning

The Halloween she was nine
my daughter agreed to the astronaut
costume. I casually drew her away
from the violent superheroes and the silly
princesses via the intriguing helmet.
Though, ultimately, the lens did not move
up and down as we had imagined. Yet she stood
with such confidence in that bright white uniform,
holding that helmet to one side and posing
one hand on her hip, just so,
so that the NASA patch would appear,
but not the US flag in the picture.
And now she is asking more and more
questions about the skies. *Did you know*
you and Mama are both Earth
signs? Did you know Great-Granny
is a Gemini? And for her Unsung Heroes
PowerPoint, she selected Katherine Johnson.
A Black women scientist, Ms. Johnson
mastered complex manual calculations
at NASA for 35 years. And when virtual
fourth grade ended, my daughter selected
the composition book with the cover
of blue skies and white constellations
for her summer journal. Even over the dinosaurs.
And now, as her dedication
to both astronomy and astrology continue,
from time to time she still asks me:
But are you sure, we cannot know,
the exact time, when I was born?

Calculate

The power of life and death is in the tongue.
—Barry C. Black, the Senate chaplain, in a prayer ending a joint session of Congress hours after a violent crowd of rioters stormed the U.S. Capitol on January 6, 2021. We watched it all unfold on the television in real time from our home in Washington D.C., six miles away.

We cannot protect our children
from all of the calculators on the internet
during their distance learning math quizzes,
or starting their own Tik-Tok accounts
without permission or even all of the adult-only websites,
until they are 18. We cannot fully protect them
from the gender binaries as only one of the teachers
says *Good morning to all my kings and queens*
and non-binary royalty. We cannot tell our children
enough times that calculators are like fire
or like our own words as the Scripture says. The fire that creates
golden brown marshmallows for our pandemic smores
in Shalini's and Smita's backyard is the very element
that is right now destroying homes in California,
and tore through our Kingston hotel, and my friend's childhood
home in New Jersey. And so, too, our words can build us
up or tear us to shreds, words like *bright light* or *difficult,*
or *Why don't you understand this? I already explained*
it three times this evening. Words that say: *We appreciate*
your passion and ethical compass, or *You are my daughter,*
and I will always love you, yes, even if you are gay,
and yes, even on the days when the math problems
are mostly wrong or mostly right.

Symmetry

As my daughter took her day two
fifth grade beginning of the year standardized
assessments on the other side
of this wall, I listened to my former boss's boss's boss
(Eric Dreiband) tell the First Circuit Appellate Court
that the US federal government no longer believes
in affirmative action. And so he says, if colleges review
the whole candidate, including race, they are engaging
in illegal, race-based discrimination. I re-read my poem
on affirmative action and wonder if that's one
I should share at an upcoming legal conference.
That poem, inspired by this line
from a job advertisement:

The candidate should hail from a well-regarded law school.

As for the fifth grade parents, we were given careful instructions
to encourage, but not to help, our children
with their standardized tests.
The school provided a handout entitled:
Supportive Phrases to Use with Students.
In the two-page document, it included versions of:

Do not help your student

four different times.
It then gave sample language
to use instead of helping
your student. For math, they suggested
we say: *Try working it out
on paper.* For reading,

they suggested we say: *Try going back
to the text.* They suggested
we say: *It's okay if you don't know
the answer.* They suggested we say: *Make a guess
and move on to the next one.* After the student completes
the assessment they suggested we say: *I'm really proud
of you. You did a great job taking your time,
showing your work, persisting
through challenging questions.*

On the other side of the wall,
I remind my daughter
to take breaks. To drink water. To eat
her green grapes. And after two days of tests,
with so many unknowable
answers, the only question
she had for me was: *What's symmetry?*

Religious, and Spiritual

At the end of all my roads
of logic and self-confidence, where all my planning
dead-ends, there and only there, there comes a time
when I am forced to say: *Give it to God.*
When one goes to pick up one's toddler daughter
in another country and the court date
was actually for another child.
When one walks oneself down Perkins Street
to find a taxi on Center Street
for an emergency surgery to remove
a soon-rupturing-cyst. I remember our activist
ancestor Eileen Fay would say, *Jesus,*
Mary, and Joseph, be with us
on our way, every summer afternoon in 1984
as we began our Chicagoland ride
to the Kennedy Park swimming pool.
When crouched on the floor of the bathroom
at the doctor's office, bleeding without end
and late to catch a flight
to take a deposition in another city,
only in these times do I remember
to be faithful. *My Lord*
is my shepherd. I shall not want. The sun
will not hurt me during the day. Nor the moon
during the night. I still recall my anger
when my favorite television program,
Little House on the Prairie, was interrupted
by my family's compulsory nightly prayers
and my forced reading of the Psalms. And now,
almost 40 years later, we stand together

in a circle, for *Appacha* to pray,
at the end of each visit home. And I still
smile with surprise every time
he says, out loud: *And dear Lord, bless Erika,
Satya, Sunu* somewhere, somehow, inside the heart
of our very long family prayer.

THREE

Some Company for Her Questions

The Boy in the Holly Berry Store

One December in the florist shop,
the boy in the holly berry store
told me I had pretty eyes.
I said thank you and meant it.
I didn't say let me tell you about sexual harassment
I didn't say I hope you don't say such
things to your co-workers
because that could be illegal
and I didn't whip out my federal employee badge
and talk to him about civil rights
for women in the workplace.

When the boy in the holly berry store
asked if my boyfriend would mind
if he spent New Year's Eve with me,
I asked if I could get my holly berry for free
since I had pretty eyes.
I didn't say what makes you assume
I have a boyfriend and not a girlfriend
and even if I had a boyfriend
what makes you think that he tells me what to do
and who to spend my time with.

When the boy in the holly berry store
said happy holidays and be safe,
I said you too and meant it.
I didn't say you know
these days my ego and my politics get entangled
in ways they never used to before.
And days when I hear rumors that

someone in Boston actually
left me, saying behind my back
that I was too fat, on those days,
the boy in the holly berry store
can get away with more.

Taxi Driver Brother Man

Winter fling and I trying to get home
Sunday night from the dyke bar.
But taxi cabs are not stopping
for Black girls who look like Black boys,
or for Indian girl in baggy pants
hanging out with Black bois,
no longer looking like attorney in suit
with white friends and briefcase.

Winter fling and I finally get a cab
and have the nerve to start kissing.
After all that is why she got on the plane
and came to this city—
no cousins that she needs to visit really.
We start kissing and Taxi Driver Brother Man
says, *I don't take that in my cab.* We stop immediately,
and we stop completely. But his disgust
too potent perhaps, Taxi Driver
Brother Man pulls over—*Just get out.*
Angry and afraid, the cold unbearable,
we wait and wait, once again.

Next day I see a brochure about how city cabs can't discriminate
on the basis of sexual orientation, or race.
Would Taxi Driver Brother Man have kicked out
a straight white kissing couple?
Don't think so. Don't think so.

Do I call the enemy, the TLC, the Taxi
and Limousine Commission

on Taxi Driver Brother Man?
The same place that takes away their licenses
for bullshit reasons?
Don't think so. Don't think so.

And would I feel the same way if my dad
was the taxi driver and the two girls kissing
were some Lower Eastside white girls?
Don't think so. Don't think so.
I might be saying, *Why they gotta disrespect
an older South Asian man with this mess?
What's wrong with them?*

I don't want to be kicked out Taxi Driver Brother Man,
and I don't want to turn you in either.

A few days later I am speaking on a panel
with Taxi Advocate Professor Man. I know I am down
for their cause completely. But what I also really want to know
is, when is Taxi Driver Brother Man gonna be down for me?

Cracked

Last week I was told about a museum with broken vases,
broken vases that were put back together using 24-karat gold,
the gold rivers making tributaries, making streams,
across the ceramic. I imagine such a reconstituted vase
would be more beautiful, even, than the original.
Many of us have someone like her, that person
who never forgives us. I don't believe in new age stuff,
mostly but today, her spirit so strong, it must be
her birthday. Another rainy February,
and three years have gone by. I am starting to believe
her line in the sand is forever, for real.

This story began 13 years ago in the village of Vellanad. After days spent seeking the elusive Calcutta gay film festival and settling for the Tagore museum, new actor and journalist friends, and a side trip to Bokaro Steel City, I gratefully returned to the softer light and the fresh green landscapes of the community center in Kerala. I return to broken flashlights and afternoon electricity failures, to fuchsia and peacock green daily wear outfits and the handsome social studies teacher in the adjoining classroom. She came out of nowhere, to rescue me from the ridiculous European flat mates who also boarded at the community guesthouse. Three months of panic and loneliness disappeared in one instant. On the first day I went with her to interview the Lady Director of the Mushroom Farm Project, and she came to my writing group with vocational students. On the second day, I asked her to stop using the word *fag,* and during dinner she asked me not to take all of the onions in the mutta curry. On the third day I took this stranger with me to Ammachi's home in Thiruvalla, three hours away by train.

After all, it was her birthday. It was February, 1995.

I asked the creepiest uncle to purchase a birthday cake,
wondering if he thought of these small favors as some penance
for all he had done to damage other cousins.
As if buying a birthday cake for the new best friend
of one of his nieces makes up for one afternoon
of *close the shutters and lay on the bed next to me*.
But the idea of laying on the bed with the shutters closed,
in the afternoon, with this particular uncle felt odd
to this eight-year-old and she did close the shutters
but then ran to the next room, and somehow escaped
what some of the others suffered. Others, who at age 25,
still lock the bedroom door, only on nights when he sleeps over.

After we ate her birthday cake, my new best friend and I
roamed among the rubber trees. We helped Ammachi get up
from her chair and made jokes as we climbed with her up to
the terrace. We said hello to the pashu in the yard and drank her
milk with our afternoon tea. We listened to the wailing songs of
morning prayer, frightened and fascinated at once by the harsh
sounds. By the time the train pulled back into Trivandrum, we
had hit one man with our water bottle and pricked another with
a safety pin when he came too close, all tricks we learned from
our cousins for times like these.

After another dinner of avial and sambar, we left the man with
the lovely patch of skin on his chest that she stared at through
dinner and planned our two-girls-alone journey through India.
We picked a fresh papaya for dessert and sat on the floor next
to the newspaper, now filled with black seeds, and mapped our
routes. I agreed to go to the Ajanta Caves and she agreed to go
to the Konark Sun Temple—and to check all the bathrooms
before I went in.

After a day at the Gujurat amusement park, we lay on the grass outside the dairy factory's housing complex and looked up at the stars. Even the sky in North India seemed different. The sky and the air and the ladies out walking, even at night, it was all so different.

As we traveled, she knew when it was time to pretend she was my girlfriend—that one Bombay dyke was overbearing on the dance floor. But she also knew when it was time to pretend she barely knew me—the Delhi non-profit cutie is calling to schedule coffee.

Like any other relationship, I fell in love with her family. Doctor Aunty climbed with us to all of the Rajasthan palaces. She came to the desserts, to the camels, to the naked ladies bathing on the side of the road. Doctor Aunty took me to church on Easter Sunday in Jaipur. Like any other relationship, she fell in love with my family. She took 100 photographs of my six-year-old cousin as he helped to prepare green beans for dinner one night in Baroda.

By the end, our day trips had taken us from day trips to Woodstock, New York, and the hills of Shimla. We bought too many sweets for the bus trip to the Taj Mahal and not enough sparkling lemonade for a day at the beach in Long Island. I went to Teaneck to hang out with her family. She yelled at me for taking too many onions from the mutta curry.

During my third apartment move in Brooklyn, she went to the hardware store three separate times for me. She waited with the movers. She took my garment rack apart and put my garment rack back together. She went through all the *Time Out New York* magazines and tore out the good articles. She met me three minutes after my first big break up. We met for Thai food in Soho and she held my hand as I sat in shock.

My winter fling built her entire Ikea desk one afternoon as we sat and giggled and watched Malayalam movies. We made real homemade chocolate cake for her birthday. She picked out the brown silk pillows, still on my couch, and she selected my first nose ring, still on my nose.

And then in one instant, sitting together
for a late lunch at a mid-town fountain
three years ago, it all fell apart. Her parting as abrupt
and surprising as her arrival. She would say I betrayed
her. She said it felt like I punched her
in the stomach. I said she had no claim
on my friend. Some days I wonder if I was wrong
and if that's one reason for my tragedy. The ministers
and therapists all say it is nonsense, but the question remains,
was it or was it not a betrayal, and does that actually matter?

Like any other break-up we divided up the spaces of the world. She got the food co-op shift and the Brooklyn meditation group. Like any other break-up I don't know what to do with her aunt's 24-karat gold earrings which are as valuable to me as the memory of our day at Spring Lake. What to do with her books, her letters, her cards, her Malayalam script writing, *snehathil*, as we both learned to write from the Vellanad Appacha. Like other break-ups, my friends run into her and I grill them for some small detail that means she still loves me. I search for any indication that she will come back.

Meanwhile, I have cobbled together some delightful and incomplete replacements. The hole she left gaping and obvious. Like any other break-up, I realize I need to put myself out there, I mean, how else do you make new friends? I review a new batch of friend candidates and decide who to recruit next. I pull the file of resumes from the folder in my head marked, *People I think I would really like but never get to hang out with.* I consider who may have the time to spare.

This one can tell me about her book of poems. This one will go on the moonlight bike ride with me in Prospect Park. This one and I chatted for four hours on a bus to DC once. This one can speak to me in Malayalam and take me to Teaneck to see her family. This one seems wary of drowning in a new friendship. This one has a mean streak; I don't like the way she talks about her friends. This one full of mystery and mischief. A decision is made that we must divide up the responsibilities among several individuals.

Like any other break-up, I hear a long-ago song and remember her laugh. I see a red and gold ceramic paisley plate and remember her face. One day in 2001 she bought some such plates off the street in Williamsburg. She had big plans to smash and destroy them and to create from the shards, a mosaic tile table. I kept thinking, we could have just eaten pisem or carrot halva or birthday cake on those stunning plates, as they were. Creating a mosaic tile table would have required reconstructing, forgiving, putting pieces back together. But she could not find enough trust, or enough gold, for such intricate projects, for such delicate, time-consuming work.

I remember her trinkets galore, antique buttons here, a color copy of an Indian miniature painting there, her golden yellow raw silk duvet cover, her teal handmade curtains, even a sewing machine, and yet seemingly no ability at all to stitch us back together. One afternoon, she called me to say she finally found the perfect milky light-green knobs for her kitchen cabinets. Somedays I think the world is divided between people who care about the design of items, like measuring cups or zippers or notebooks, and those who don't. She was satisfied only with very specific things, things of beauty and delight.

She surprised me with a Ganesh statue
on our last day together in Kerala. Our Christian aunties
looked on and frowned at the two silly American

girls. They laughed and repeated what they had said
all year long, *koot-ay-eee*, one Malayalam word
that all by itself means, *it's clear to anyone*
observing that a real friendship has been formed
here, so quickly and so strong, like synergy,
two-girls-alone became at once one team,
and anyone observing could just feel
the energy, the loyalty. She must have felt all of this
smashed to pieces. These pieces, I can only imagine
these smashed-up pieces, on her dresser
in a Ziploc bag, against the perfect lavender wall
that we painted together one Sunday afternoon.

Where the Wild Things are

You said, *Sure, let's paint over the green
cabinets of our East Flatbush home, and just erase
all the memories.* Your sister's junior high
attendance award still stands on what should serve as our home
altar. The man of the house left before you turned four
but it's still your job to toss out his magazines
from the garage. The lidless white paper box
with the last purse your mother carried continually moves
to the center of any room. This box with her students'
handwritten *We will miss you*s, with rainbows and flowers
painted on the outside. Yesterday, you pulled that box out
again so you could paint the inside of your childhood
closet to fit our daughter's things. This last
leather purse your mother carried, again becomes our center-
piece. As we select baby's bedtime
story, I stare at this purse that I am afraid
to touch. These countless keepsakes that drive
and disturb your hesitant paint strokes.

Fake Roof Deck Makeovers in Brooklyn

(from my email inbox)

Hey, I'm working on a TV project and we're looking for a roof deck in Brooklyn to makeover. Ideally, 12x16 or so. If they don't really need a makeover, we can fake for the cameras. Know anyone who has something?

Boxing-up the China

In the space between the green kitchen
and the grill lies your mother's dining
room. Spilled pushpins on the floor, a worn
hammock that could not hold me. Encyclopedias,
unopened cook books, the failed marriage
china. On the other side of the room,
a broken desk chair, a printer that works
erratically. You once made the dining table my
home office. With an official sign. With my
name. But even now, I can only see your image
far away, blurry through a window that won't stay
open. Through the smoky air, I still see you though:
head down, tending to coals. My head down
too, tending to too many soiled
dishes. Between us, on a silver tray,
and too often forgotten, a feast:
grilled fish, onions, red peppers, and peaches.

I grow fond of the kitchen cabinet doors that swing open unless we secure them by inserting something between the two handles

This kitchen's green paint, somewhere between
mint and fluorescent was surely a fresh
idea back then. The girl who has built frame houses
by the waters of the Mississippi, and in Oakland, is now frozen
and still. This one who has completed gut renovations
on bathrooms near the Hudson. In three minutes she could fix
this disconnect, but that would mean we begin
the erasure. Before this chopstick, we used a plastic
fork. Before that, a thick rubber band. Before that, the green
doors just swung open, announcing every morning:
all the favored teas were gone,
the jasmine, the chai, the peppermint. Only
one box of decaffeinated discount tea
remained—unopened and sealed.

Fake Drinking Wells in Kerala

Some NRIs who are building
retirement homes in gated communities
in India are insisting on digging wells in the front yard,
simply for the sake of nostalgia. But my own parents
grew up with wells in front and outhouses
behind their homes. I am but one generation removed
from village homes in Thiruvalla, ones that began without
running water, without a toilet inside. Do we have enough
distance yet for this to count as nostalgia,
or would it simply remind
us of the inconvenience?

Practice raking leaves or sweeping to remind oneself of the feeling of engaging in work that knows no end

From a list of Buddhist tips regarding maintaining a neat and mindful home

It took three months to replace the broken
doorknob on the front door. Every time I entered,
struggle. Every departure, a fight
for closure. Purchasing a new doorknob
took minutes, installing it, just half
of one weekday evening. The solid feel
of the new doorknob, a small kind
of salvation. With every entrance, calm,
with every exit, the relief
of normalcy. In this home float
at least three ghosts and 100 broken
doorknobs. With each small repair,
an acknowledgment of what can be
fixed. With each remaining brokenness, a despair
that knows no end. But the pleasant weight of it
in my hand, the strong click
of a lock that fits, the sureness,
unhesitating. I want to hug
the front door for waiting
with its patient brokenness
for all those months. A few days later,
two cabinets fell right off
the basement tenant's kitchen walls. By the time
we awoke, she showed us the cans
of soup, corn, and beans,
and how they lay scattered
all around her kitchen floor.

Apartment 5J

This time we carry collards from the garden,
raisins from the farmer's market.
Didn't buy lunch once this week.

Kept getting promoted until she didn't.
Mothers all ask the same questions.

The bathroom is already tired.
My coat, scarf, and haircut remind you.

As requested I came in
to Granny's nighttime world
of red flannel pajamas and missing
front teeth.

Another apartment in Brooklyn
Another apartment in Brooklyn.
Another apartment in Brooklyn.

Though none of the furniture fits yet,
an evening flute still plays
scales in the distance.

Ode to the Broken Printer, Three Printers Ago

It's almost like they need names.
The broken printer from when we lived
in the Argonne. The broken printer
from the apartment by Ginger's in Park
Slope. The newly broken printer
just bought during the global pandemic.
The broken printer from East Flatbush,
and this one, from the Fort Greene studio.
E likes to repair things. She is pro-composting
and anti-landfills. And when something breaks
she keeps it, just to see what can be done.
With a reluctant nod to her values, I had kept this broken
printer much longer than planned. When she came over
one evening I said, I was done. She had
one more evening to fix the printer. In my studio
apartment with a three-year-old, we had no space
for broken things. One week before,
our friend had stayed overnight with our daughter
and we enjoyed our first weekend away
after becoming parents. E had told my parents
long ago that she was planning to marry me. I was utterly lost
at why I hadn't come back from the North Fork
of Long Island, an engaged person. That didn't help
my mood and increased the pitch that the broken
printer had to go. I gave her one last chance
and fell asleep on the couch. One hour later she wheeled over
on the office chair and woke me up. In jagged
lines going all over the page, complete with messed-up
lettering and too-light toner, printed over and over
on the page, there it was. Her repeated test-print:
Will You Marry Me?

Radical Love-Building Sustainable Open Relationships Workshop

Six and a half years later she finally consented
to attend the workshop.
Day after Christmas, rainy winter night
deceptively cold stinging rain hits
our faces. They said it was over 40 degrees,
and no one brought hats or gloves.

We enter Bluestockings and see three dogs roaming
around the room. One light brown dog with a quick
step and wagging tail. A full-bodied, slow-
moving blond-haired dog and
one short-haired dark-brown beauty.
The three doggies follow her around, sniffing
the little bag of cookies from Dean and DeLuca.
I asked her to eat beforehand or least bring a snack—
I wanted her to be in the best possible frame
of mind. Perhaps she would think *open relationship*
and think *chocolate chip cookies*.

But even one dog would have been
too much to risk,
given the intense allergies.
She is fidgeting and annoyed
at this loosey-goosey establishment.
What kind of place lets in this many dogs?
I inquire and the shopkeeper clarifies:
One dog actually lives here, and
no, we have no policy regarding dogs except to say that
people can bring them in.

She is not sneezing yet but
she knows she will start if she stays,
and she cannot risk it. She believes
she can predict all that is on the way. We agree she can leave,
and I will take good notes. In my head
there are three choices and none of them good
ones. She knows that once she starts
wheezing, she could encounter a full-scale attack.
She says she is just not buying it,
that people can do this, and
I am standing at the cash register, wallet in hand.

Heavy Wash Cycle

In the midst of a Boston blizzard, I still took two trains
and walked 10 minutes through the snow. The pull of it,
that draw of someone gorgeous and inconsistent
with her kindness. And now, I can still win over
the building mate who left me a nasty note
on the laundry room dryer. Quarantine
insisted all our pillows needed washing. Only one
dryer with enough capacity. I pulled out her dry sheets
and duvet covers, placed them up top. I knew it was risky.
Upon my return, a note. A *how dare you* note. An *in the middle
of this pandemic* note. A *now I have to wash
and dry my sheets again* note. I told my daughter,
She's right. We should have waited. On our next trip
to the laundry room, I took a hand-painted
ladybug card from the Burlington artists' fair,
taped it on the dryer. *You are so right.
I am so sorry. Here's $10 for your extra washing and drying.*
Two weeks later, my daughter noticed a response.
To the person who left me the kind note. *Thank you.
Hope your family is keeping well in these times.*
Sincerely, Alexandra. And $5 change. I already know
that winning over tough people is my superpower. Even still,
some other things are forever unknowable.
Why won't the neighbor take her clothes out
from the one large community dryer
on time? Why wouldn't she ever come to me
in the middle of those Boston blizzards?

Rebuilding Efforts II

A new level of compassion
for Eliza in Hamilton,
sitting on the bench, burning
her letters. Writing herself out
of the narrative. Because while Hamilton had one
kind of integrity, he failed
at so many others. A deeper
understanding of all who stay,
despite friends saying: *Wait, hold on,*
he did what? Mistrust cuts
arrogance with a chainsaw, confidence
with a machete. A punch to the gut, and we
are never the same. I replay the whole story
five times at any mention of it. First, I find
the box of it in its woodshed
with bamboo floors and heavy
navy curtains. It is always dark
inside. Only a small candle burns
at the far end of the room. In the middle
of the floor is a magnificent blood-red
cabinet, the size of your whole
body, with three locks. Inside,
three shelves. On the top shelf, in a gold
frame, the letter I found
two years ago. Frayed edges visible
even within the frame. On the second shelf,
a tape-recorder poised to play
the entire aftermath. I rewind the cassette
over and over, to the therapist
reassuring: *This was not an affair,*

though a series of bad and hidden choices.
We join the ranks of all who engage in endless
repair. We create a plan. The cabinet will remain
in the shed. I will avoid it
as much as possible. You will not add
any items to it. You promise to send alerts
if there is ever danger nearby.
For while our vows did not mention
either fidelity or forever, we distinctly
promised each other compassion.

Ninety-Five

When I ask my Facebook friends, who mostly don't know her,
to send cards for her 95th, I hesitate to write: and she will open
them on her birthday. But I write it anyway. My partner confides
that when Granny is reaching a big birthday, she just hopes
that she will make it. And in writing this poem I feel afraid
to put these words down onto paper, too. Last week
Granny said any kind of cake would be just fine, as long
as it comes with a trip home to Barbados. And while there's no trip
to Barbados this year, the carrots are ready
to be grated into her cake, the packages of cream cheese
ready to be whipped into homemade frosting.
We will all take Wednesday off, finding some place
that is outdoors but still away from all the people.
We are wondering if she will keep the mask on her face.
I am wondering what color she will select for her home pedicure.
I am wondering if she will say I thank you very much
when I am done with her fingers and her toes. I know
one day I will miss her singing random lines of hymns that ring
through our apartment. He taught me how, to watch and pray,
and live rejoicing, every day. Happy day. Happy day. When Jesus
washed my sins away. I won't miss dragging up
the large boxes of her necessary supplies from the lobby
every few weeks or the days when we have strangers
in our home as substitute health aides. I will miss
asking our daughter to take Great-Granny some portion
of anything that we cook at home, even if
she has already eaten. I won't miss always sitting
in the back seat for every family trip. I will miss her
laugh. I will miss when we poke gentle fun at my spouse—
her granddaughter. I will miss us playfully teasing

our daughter, her great-granddaughter.
Back during our third non-date date in August 2008
my now-spouse said, *Come, let me take you by our house.* I sat
quietly on the couch, as far away as I could
from her roommate, Granny. This elder who had lost
her only daughter just one year before and was now
stuck with her youngest granddaughter. This elder
who had to start relying on this 27-year-old kid
to make all her salads, to complete all her paperwork,
to take her to all her medical appointments.
This kid who hadn't lived at home for years,
who was used to leaving town
at a moment's notice. With only a medium
backpack. And now this kid needs a vehicle,
and one big enough to carry it all. Not just a trunk,
but one large enough to accommodate
the walker, the suitcases, the wheelchair,
and the diapers. And now, 12 years later,
even though Great-Granny sometimes asks:
Why are those two men kissing when *Modern Family*
comes on the television, she also refers to me,
her granddaughter's wife, as her own beloved grandkid too.

.

Mattina Mia

—Italian for "My Morning," the name of the Syrian man's hair salon near Dupont Circle, Washington, D.C.

It was Mattina Mia, all sunrise and cold, that dawn
of walking without one's senses
awake. I stumble in that glorious
in-between state. The one before
you remember all the reasons why
morning bliss cannot remain.
The sun almost up, but not quite,
the wind, the skies, the world feels grand
and full of possibility. Mattina Mia, I walk.
To see God in the sky at 6 a.m. is more possible,
there are less people in her way.

Inside the fitness studio, a girl's shirt reads:
You had me at namaste.

The first time I heard namaste, I was six-years-old. Imagine it was my first trip to India to meet my grandparents, my aunts, my uncles, and my cousins. I still have the vaccination mark, this bodily mis-marker on my left shoulder, that they gave me in Jamaica to prepare for the trip. It marks me as from the auntie generation, as perhaps not born in the US, though that's not the case.

I must have been six or seven. I must have seen the Air India flight attendants make a bowing gesture when they uttered this sound—*namaste*. I often befriended the flight attendants as I had no siblings and my parents were frequently arguing above my head. Whenever I tried to involve myself they would say: *If there's something you need to know, we will tell you.*

Another time, I sat at the back with the flight attendants and explained Quakerism, as I was wearing my *Quakers are Friends* T-shirt from summer camp. *We believe in peace, we are against the death penalty, we are against war, we know everyone has an inner light.* They must have bowed to the divinity within me, as I did to them, and meant it.

And somehow that girl's shirt made my Mattina less Mia. It made it more America's. Her T-shirt took my trips to India to be with Ammachi and made it an ethnic design on her yoga mat. She took my feeling so different as the only immigrants in small-town Ohio and made it her fashion accessory. She took the hatred of immigrants with accents and made it the design on her gym bag. She took me back to the "looks like Hindi" lettering on the wall at the Crunch gym in Lower Manhattan. She took me back to the Ganesha Gods doing yoga with their blue god friends at the yoga studio in Washington, D.C. Less Mattina Mia by the moment.

Leaving the gym that morning,
an older Black woman stood
puzzled next to the parking meter.
Knowing nothing about solving
such problems I really wanted
to just walk by. She was looking around
for someone, anyone, to provide
some company for her questions.
Her question was simple
enough: *Do you think this meter
is for this space?* I gave her my best guess
and that's all she needed,
just someone to say:
*Yes, I think you have it
right.* And with her smile,
my Mattina Mia became
more mine again.

And then, arriving home at 7 a.m., there is always one
dog and one human in the elevator going up. The specific
pairing changes, but always one set. The dog
is always wagging with joy, savoring
that moment between the morning walk
and morning breakfast. There is no better
moment in their lives. And when I say hello
to the doggies and smile, the humans always beam.
This way we all beam, at seeing love expressed
to another being we love.

Shelter-In-Place

Part One: Oath of Office

I pledge allegiance to the church basement meetings,
to the chairs in a circle. To the volunteer lawyers at the airport
and the ones running to file in the federal courts. I pledge
allegiance to keeping my paycheck, until I have a new one.
I pledge allegiance to my child—to seeing her before
she goes to bed at night, at least some of the time. I pledge
allegiance to poetry, and to protecting
my staff. To standing in the hallway
with management, quietly grieving. I pledge
allegiance to loneliness, to only crying
during the commute. I pledge allegiance to vacations
over objects, to experiences over things. But I also pledge
allegiance to nice things, the smallest things, to flowers
for the boss on our worst days, and flowers for all
of us too. I pledge allegiance to facing conflict head-on
and choosing our battles. I pledge allegiance to the organizers,
to the ones moving through the tears, to people sitting around
a table and writing our poems anyway.

Part Two: Elk Hunting

Small talk before the first meeting with new leadership
focused on their failed elk hunting trip. Unexpected knee-deep
snow kept all the elk hidden away. Hunters disappointed,
they returned to camp. Mother Universe protected her kin,
this time. We pray for the same. A year closes
with all our dread sitting right beside us. The next morning
the radio journalist mentions an increase in hate

crime and rebel resistance. I cannot make out
which country she names.

Part Three: Questions to a Place

I am wondering if the whole country is turning into 1979,
small-town Ohio again. A white gazebo in the center of town,
and one traffic light. It's a 12-mile journey to the grocery store.
Friday evenings we head to Hillsboro to Frisch's Big Boy for ice
cream sundaes once Uncle finishes his shift. The farmers asked
my father to pray for rain or sun, depending. Mostly, I claim
the lilac bushes and the tire swing. And even though we have
tomato plants and three kinds of roses, something still doesn't
smell right. With our American flag in the window, we try to
belong to a place where there are none of us. We left that behind
but now it is 2017. America, will you try to call me Sue again?
Will you tell me that I speak English well again? America, will
you ask me for my papers again? Will you say again, *I don't know
where you came from, but in this country we have freedom of speech* when
I tell the three male attorneys to stop sexually harassing a young
woman? America, will you yell to me out your car window on
College Avenue: *Hey, nigger?* America, will you ask if I am Hindi
and then ask me about Indian restaurants again? America, does
my spouse no longer have a pronoun again? America, are we
going back to: *You're pretty, well, for an Indian.* To: *No, really though,
where are you from?*

Self-Portrait as a Vase of Half-Wilted Flowers

HHS Employee Bathroom, 200 Independence Avenue

That January, my body impulsively
created a ritual of rearranging
the flowers. One way
to cope with that parallel
sorting of sorts. A daily standing
by the sink, eyes in the mirror,
separating. Dead leaves from live
branches. A daily negotiation—
can any of this still be good? What parts ready
to be trashed, overdue in truth. A constant
questioning of what's worth
saving? A continual reassurance
of something still yellow,
some capacity left to bring joy,
just because. This need to tend,
tend oneself. To separate what's gone
and what's still available,
what's of service. Wilted leaves
with the green though, clinging.
Always a surprise. How much is left
in the end. You will be retained
for now, for one more
round. The woman at the flower
stand by the metro called these black-eyed
Susans. Says they'll last. And a few of last week's
daisies, still here too
refusing to die.

First Quarantine Poem

1. How to Wash Your Hands

First, find a song.
Then double-check how many seconds to scrub.
Don't forget underneath your fingernails.
Don't forget your wrists. Include your palms
and each finger, one by one.
Remember integrity.
Repeat after the morning walk.
Repeat after you pick up the mail.
Repeat after you wash the produce.
Repeat after you wash the milk carton.
Repeat after you use the bathroom.
Repeat after you get this week's piano sheet
music printed downstairs at the leasing office.
Repeat after you take out the recycling.
Repeat after you make lunch for the family.
Repeat after you retrieve the package from the lockers.
Repeat after you return from the building's laundry room.
Repeat before you start making dinner.
Remember integrity.
Remember what is at stake.
Repeat after the morning walk.

2. How to Avoid that Place called Panic

First, find a song.
The song is entitled: We have survived hard things before.
The song is sub-titled: So many are suffering, and in worse ways.
The chorus reminds you there is help
out there, if it comes to that.
The chorus reminds you, you can still be helpful

to others, even when you are worried.
Remember integrity.
Repeat after the morning walk.
Repeat before you start the day's work.
Repeat after you teach your daughter the idea of decimals.
Repeat after your spouse's salary is cut
to a fraction. Repeat after you avoid
your parents' calls that week.
Repeat after you teach your daughter about the Battle
of Bunker Hill. And the Revolutionary War.
Repeat after you learn that your friend may be laid off.
Repeat after your office issues fact
sheets on how this all impacts women so much
more. On Black women, so much more. Repeat because it's not
an anecdote. Repeat because it's not anecdotal.
Repeat after you press: Okay, yes, I am still
watching. It is 1 a.m. and I am still
watching. Repeat when the four health aides'
livelihoods are in our hands. Repeat when our own health
feels in the balance. Remember integrity.
Remember what is at stake.
Repeat after the morning walk.

Rebuilding Efforts III

I went to Facebook to share the news
about the bird building a nest
inside our patio bird feeder. One evening,
we gently removed the twigs and placed them
in a careful pile on the patio floor. The next morning,
all those twigs, all of them,
were right back in our bird feeder. And now
the people want to know
what kind of bird is taking over
our bird feeder as its own private home. A house
sparrow, the internet confirms. My colleague chimes in,
when this happened to her,
she just gave up and purchased a new mailbox.

And the internet also warns: *Once birds begin*
to build a home, they are loathe to leave it.

Inside our home, I wonder how can it be
that after finally viewing our wedding footage,
this does not lead to love. And though I dramatically trashed
the romance books that did not kill our spark. Most of the time,
it's as if she wants to share rosemary
crackers and to try new cheeses. And in the morning,
she makes us all blueberry crepes.

And then one day on a stage, someone told her story,
about a different kind of fire. With an algebra
that just works in the body, differently.
Only then, did I begin
to understand that there are things

I will never understand. That
some things that appear the most personal
are not to be taken personally.

And now, when I witness her,
building things on the patio
I send for her one of the four
tumblers of homemade
milkshake. And I always ask the child
delivering the treats, to *Wait, wait,*
come back, so that I can always make sure
to sprinkle nutmeg on her portion too.

Gratitude List

Thank you to myself for not responding to the guy from college who wrote on my FB wall *what do you mean* after I said to him: *I hope you count yourself among the feminists.*

Thank you for the feminists.

Thank you for the bright carrots, the lemons, and the roasted garlic.

Thank you for my daughter's notes. Thank you for my daughter's questions.

Thank you for the spouse who still makes me laugh in that smile and gently roll my eyes way, almost daily.

Thank you for the kitchen, right after we sweep every night.

Thank you for the poet who decided to write a thank-you note to her friend after he died. Because what else can one do.

Thank you for family PE time and all the many people involved in putting together an online yoga class and an online cardio class and an online meditation session.

Thank you for the drive for one more Zoom—because the Indigo Girls are singing, because it's the church meeting, because it's the friends who used to do Brooklyn game nights, because it's the junior choir practice, because Heather is turning 60, because Annie is graduating, because these poets have new books out, because it's Naomi reading poems, because it's Joy reading poems.

Thank you for the bus drivers, nurses, and the grocery store check-out cashiers. For the home healthcare workers in our living room every day, and the other ones who are now out of work.

Thank you for cake. For the first time making coconut cake from scratch. For lemon cake with curd filling but not great icing that time because were out of confectioners' sugar that day. Thank you for the chocolate cake that is on the agenda for next time.

Thank you for the laundry room. With its *Mask Required* sign and with the others standing as far away from us as they can.

Thank you for solidarity. For those saying this is not the fault of Asian Americans. For the bystander trainings and for all those who intervene.

Thank you for my child's questions about resurrection.

Thank you for the flowers that have all come and gone.

Thank you for the plants that do their very best to keep growing.

.

Third Quarantine Poem

Our second 500-piece puzzle is almost complete. We know
the backstories of all the contestants on *The Voice*. And
on *American Idol.* A friend texts for a rare daytime chat. At 4 p.m.
she tells me her organization is planning layoffs. We practice
for the child's weekly Zoom piano lesson. I try to play
"Say Something (I'm Giving Up On You)" on the piano.
We call to ensure that our Chicago family is staying at home.
We make coconut layer cake. For the first time. We find
all of the lost watercolors. Someone I used
to work with dies. We make sure Great-Granny stays
home. Only the most careful one among us goes
outside. And only for medicine. And only to the grocery
store. We pray for the essential workers and push
for their rights. We scrub everything hard, twice,
with soap. Each one of the oranges,
and apples, and sweet potatoes.

Wish

The poem says hey you did this *ars poetica* thing
before without knowing it. Remember that poem
about contemplating risk and another that asked
if lost embryos were worth a poem
and another about being asked to represent
South Asian lesbians at the Boston community event,
but in five minutes or less.

And now, the poem wishes
still. The poem refuses
to give up, or try harder, or leave.
The poem is at a standstill with itself.

The poem fights
to be lightweight yet strong
enough to carry everything.
Like a hold-everything
handbag with a silky smooth zipper.

My friend says don't take your children to that movie,
the monsters look real. The poem is wondering
about real monsters. Real monsters like an email
with the subject line, *pregnant again,* or
another average evaluation, or a critique
of the tea or the toast.

The poem should really be more
about service, no, about activism, no, about art, no,
about God, no. The poem dreams of politics,
radically nuanced through words strung together

like small white lights in a darkening
room on a Sunday afternoon.

The poem is distracted though
when a colleague turns 51
and shares his cake. The poem is stunned
by this piece of cake with
a white flower so large and so precise,
it causes everything else in my office
that afternoon to stop.

The poem wants to be that kind of flower, no,
to gesture to that flower, no,
to be the talent, or even simply the drive.
The drive that made someone out there,
just wish for this moment, this.

Tell us your reason for canceling.*

This is needed to complete your cancellation.

1. Found a different accommodation option
2. Unable to travel due to restrictions related to coronavirus
3. Change in the number or needs of travelers
4. Change of dates or destination
5. Made bookings for the same dates—canceled the ones I
   don't need
6. Personal reasons/trip called off
7. None of the above

When Expedia wanted to know
all the reasons why we were no longer
going to Staunton, Virginia, it was similar
to the LGBTQ women's survey inquiring:
How did your family of origin react to you being LGBTQ?
Check all that apply. Never enough space
even with a box marked other and space
to write something in. How do you mark
off a box called sleet?
How do you mark off that, until recently,
the best hotel in Staunton was named after Stonewall
Jackson, and this was the straw
that decided it. I decided to just give up witnessing
One of the greatest Main Streets in America,
per *Travel & Leisure.* Instead we defaulted
to Richmond, thinking it's a city, thinking we have friends
there, thinking most of the monuments have been caused
to fall. Not knowing some residents have petitioned
the Virginia Supreme Court to keep the Robert E. Lee statue
still erect. The paper reports the justices asked no questions

as the State argued that it does have the power
to take this statue down. And so upon our visit
we paid our respects to the BLM tent where folks
sat vigil. To the graffiti all over the statue, to the messages
that we are here, present and protesting.
Meanwhile, the paper reports that a judge ordered
a Virginia school district to reinstate the teacher
who refused to use trans students'
correct gender pronouns. Meanwhile, our teachers
are being fired for teaching the truth
about slavery. Tell us why any of these monuments
that maintain defiance to the notion
of a country that includes all of us
are still standing. Our country of critical race
theorists, yes, and gender justice activists, yes,
and teachers who will resist and still teach the truth,
yes, so that maybe one day, our children
can finally break this nation open.

Things I Didn't Know I Loved

The stack of books, always staring me down.

Watching the children's movie, not once, but twice.

An ex-friend reaching out, even though we will not connect.

The memory of Sapna, on top of the sadness.

Watching the evening's world news with my daughter. Her crush on the anchor man.

Routinely wearing pajama bottoms for big meetings during the pandemic.

Tennis drills outside at age 48.

Age 48.

Middle management.

Pistachio ice cream.

Glitter nail polish, but only if the glitter is gold.

Krittika's borrowed choker necklace, to go with the black and gold salwar.

Quarantine.

Chatting with Jeffrey, all night long, after stopping by his dorm to borrow 10 CDs.

Still holding on to my many cousins who missed my wedding.

The garden in Fort Greene. Planting flowers. Learning about mulch from Oza.

Chatting in the basement, doing laundry side by side with that landlord's wife.

The coffeeshop in Brooklyn,

the one that never had the things I wanted from its menu.

Write a poem in which you show love toward someone who isn't usually shown love, or a specific kind of love you'd wish they'd receive

The Honor Roll is for students who earn a grade of B- or higher in all classes. The Principal's Honor Roll is for students who earn a grade of A- or higher in all classes. – Middle School Handbook, page 16

What if middle schools
rewarded students for effort,
for the hours put into understanding
the idea of ratios or dialogue
related punctuation. What if they disbanded
tracking, and the whole Honor Roll, too.
What if everyone could run
on the track and field team.
What if we said: *Good job,*
instead of: *Wait, you didn't.*
What if we caught her,
daily, doing something right.
What if we caught her
providing Great-Granny some tenderness.
What if we caught her
one day, brushing without a reminder.
What if the world promised to scaffold
all multi-step assignments.
What if something could come easy.

What if all of the *good for foodies* restaurants
were required to be mobility accessible.

What if all of the new apartments
weren't reserved for *young professionals*.
What if the ADA made entities
pay. No, I mean, really pay.
What if we could take Great-Granny
out, anytime, anywhere in the country
without five *call back when*
the manager is here telephone calls.
What if events always provided ASL?
What if we could, two weeks after her vaccine,
all impromptu, just take Great-Granny
out for a meal, and to enjoy
live music at the arts center?

What might happen to your writing if you considered all your poems to be love poems, which are also political poems?

The three poems I have removed, would become forever gone. (Thank you, Jericho Brown.)

Years of missing
poems would find themselves.

Without question, grace.

More, open spaces.

Forgiveness, finally,
would land its starring role.

Make Yourself at Home

Ro's extra bedroom on the second floor in South Plainfield

Port Antonio, Jamaica, the verandah with chimes at our Quaker parsonage

Half of DJ Rekha's living room in the South Slope, curtained off

The Black Violin concert with Sierra

Portland hammock, in the backyard, after days in Manzanita

Quaker Youth Pilgrimage, even seven days hiking in the Cascade Mountains

Daisy's auntie's open kitchen with large windows with views of Lake Michigan

Amita's couch in Boston (after the big emergency surgery)

Alice's extra bike and attic bedroom in England, after a semester in Jerusalem

Robin's aunts' South End home (after our first time at that Boston dyke club)

Niagara Falls (an anticipatory sort of honeymoon)

That second picture of Baby V, in her yellow-green dress

You guys are doing a great job with her

The Chennai Radisson and its reliable internet

Vegetable biryani and salmon curry from Marie's Amma in Teaneck

The temporary offices at Varick, but only when they refill the water coolers

Poonam's helper's omelets in Delhi, our first time with fresh cilantro

Leave your MFA comps books here, it's walking distance to the PATH stop in Jersey City

Cape May babymoon at the Star Inn and even the next night, camping in the rain

Rearranging the Furniture

This is a found poem, or a community poem, created from phrases including from "How You Eat A Kiwifruit" & "Untitled Visions" by Robalu Gibson at Split this Rock's October 7, 2015 writing workshop. Dedicated with gratitude to Camisha Jones, Regie Cabico, and to everyone connected to the organization, Split This Rock.

Shield your child's eyes. No one to pass
judgment anymore. Do not toss out
the strange bouquet. I can hear you,
you can stop shouting now. I lifted
an arm, to signify the range
of human voice. Somewhere in the week,
a detour from grief. Porch
watch, pale sunlight. Muddy
river swamps. Faint mist thundering
while flames sting. Crimson sun,
inhale. In we go, dangled
under the stars.

Author Notes

Malayalam is the language of the state of Kerala, India, and I grew up with this language in my home alongside English. In India there are over twenty languages, and this is the only one I sort of know. There are a few Malayalam words included in some of these poems.

Six poems in this collection resulted from writing prompts from Leila Chatti during the June 2020 "Praise in Hard Times" virtual course through the Provincetown Fine Arts Center. These include: "Distance Learning," "Religious, and Spiritual," "Ode to the Broken Printer, Three Printers Ago," "Heavy Wash Cycle," "Ninety-five," and "Things I Didn't Know I Loved."

The ending of the "Wish" poem takes inspiration from Marie Howe's poem, "The Gate."

Two of the later poems in the book ("Write a Poem…" and "What might happen…") are entitled with writing prompts provided by Chen Chen during a September 2021 Kundiman Zoom Workshop. I would love to read your responses to either of these prompts, and you are invited to send them my way via the message function on my website, www.sunuchandy.net. I would love to bring your poems into the rooms during future poetry readings, and hope we can continue connecting and building community, including in this way.

A final note on the title and how it might be translated into Malayalam, with a special shout-out to Professor Roger Sedarat at CUNY Queens College and our "Craft of Literary Translations" class. As I was considering options for this translation, I had a WhatsApp discussion with my cousin Saira in Kerala in 2021 about possible words in Malayalam that might capture the meaning of my title best. Since there are many words for friendship and kinship in Malayalam, I wanted her insights as to the nuances and connotations of a range of such words. We first considered *Ente Priya Mithram*, meaning *My dear friend* which had a nice connection to Mitraniketan, the community center where I once volunteered in Kerala. And, like that, we considered a few such words back and forth. When we got to *Ente Priya Sakhakale*, she explained: "Since half of the time we have a communist government here, it means leftist too, and it also means, a band of like-minded people who are there for each other." That one felt closer. And then, eventually, we considered *Ente Priya Snehithare*, meaning *My people, the ones I love.*

Acknowledgements

Thank you to the editors of the following publications for giving some of the poems in this collection their first home, some of the poems in earlier versions or with different titles.

"Just Act Normal," "Morning, at the Lodge," "Rebuilding Efforts," "Picking up Linzer Torte Cookies for the Quaker Potluck," "Onam in Manhattan," "All Rise," and "Third Quarantine Poem" are included in *The Penguin Book of Indian Poets, 2022.*

"All Rise," published as "Hey, Thanks for Being Nice (what the Whole Foods grocery delivery guy said to my friend Pia)," AAWW, *The Margins*, included in "Bangladesh: A Thousand Words," April 24, 2014.

"Divestment," *Beltway Poetry Quarterly*, Volume 16:4, Fall 2015.

"First Quarantine Poem," Split This Rock, October 2020.

"Just Act Normal," *Beltway Poetry Quarterly*, Volume 16:4, Fall 2015.

"Kasthaputta Vanhu," *Beltway Poetry Quarterly*, Volume 16:4, Fall 2015.

"Kasthaputta Vanhu," *The Long Devotion: Poets Writing Motherhood*, University of Georgia Press, 2022.

"Knowledge," *Poets on Adoption*, May 2011.

"Lodge," *Beltway Poetry Quarterly*, Volume 16:4, Fall 2015. (Now entitled "Morning, at the Lodge")

"Practice raking leaves or sweeping to remind oneself of the feeling of engaging in work that knows no end," *Nimrod International Journal of Prose and Poetry*, Fall/Winter 2021 issue, Awards 43.

"Rearranging the Furniture," AAWW's *The Margins*, August 2016.

"Rebuilding Efforts," *Asian American Literary Review*, Volume 2, Issue 1.5, Fall 2011.

"Rest," AAWW's *The Margins*, August 2016. (Now entitled "Apartment 5J")

"Salvation Army," *Beltway Poetry Quarterly*, Volume 16:4, Fall 2015.

"Shelter In Place," *Plume*, October 2017.

"Sleet," included in "Desi Phobias," *India Currents*, March 15, 2022.

"Things I Didn't Know I Loved," *Washington Writers' Publishing House*, January 2023.

"Too Pretty," Split This Rock's *The Quarry: A Social Justice Poetry Database*, July 2016.

"To Satya From Satya," *Mom Egg Review*, March 2017.

Gratitudes

Thank you to the many communities of writers/activists where I have found inspiration and encouragement including: the Earlham College Women of Color Writing Group, the vocational students at Mitraniketan in Kerala, India, the South Asian Women for Action (SAWA) in Boston and the Desh Pardesh festival in Toronto, Sister Bisi's Women of Color writing groups in Brooklyn, the Queens College (CUNY) MFA Program, the poetry covenant group at All Soul's Unitarian Church, the community of Split This Rock, and the Unicorn Authors Club (including the crucial Early Birds subgroup). Thank you also to our independent bookstores for creating such important literary, community, and activist spaces.

Thank you to Regal House Publishing for this incredible honor of working together, including to my kind and brilliant editors, Jaynie Royal and Pam Van Dyk, as well as to C. B. Royal for designing the cover. A big thank you also goes to Martha Kalin, Regal House's Terry J. Cox Poetry Award winner from 2019, for selecting my manuscript for publication.

Thank you to my incredible cover artist Ragni Agarwal for taking my cold-call email and being open to this collaboration after I fell in love with her gorgeous art. Check out and support Ragni's art though her website: www.ragniagarwal.com and on social media, including on Instagram (@Ragni_Agarwal_). I first came to learn of Ragni's art when it was included in an email from SAADA, the South Asian American Digital Archives. I am grateful for the groundbreaking work of this organization and for their Co-founder and Executive Director, Samip Mallick. SAADA is a community-based culture change organization ensuring that South Asian Americans are included in the American story: past, present, and future. Check out and support SAADA at www.saada.org.

The creation of the poems in this book were supported in countless ways by the encouragement from many dear friends, too many to name, but special thanks goes out to Jeffrey Perkins for reading multiple drafts of this manuscript. Special thanks for their time, expertise, encouragement, inspiration, support, poem prompts, MFA reference letters, blurbs and/ or invitations to readings also go out to: Marie Varghese, Allisonjoy, Minal Hajratwala, Jaishri Abichandani, JP Howard, Rigoberto Gonzalez, Aracelis Girmay, Swati Khurana, Sister Bisi Ideraabdullah, Tracy K. Smith, Nicole Cooley, Kimiko Hahn, Roger Sedarat, Rajiv Mohabir, Regie Cabico, Kazim Ali, Purvi Shah, Lauren K. Alleyne, Naomi Jackson, Leila Chatti, Chen Chen, Fatima Goss Graves, Uma Iyer, Stacey Stevenson, Jen Soriano, Lauren R. Taylor, Tyler French, Rasha Abdulhadi, Kim Roberts, Leeya Mehta, Gowri Koneswaran, Elizabeth Toledo, Loretta Kane, Olympia Feil and Gabrielle Cicio.

Finally, my gratitude goes out to my kiddo, Satya, for all the laughs, and for making my dreams come true, so many times over. She is more than enough, and loved without condition, and always will be. My gratitude goes to my spouse, Erika Symmonds, for coming back time and time again, and for fixing all of our printers. She is known for her love language of only "practical gifts," for rising and meeting the day, and for world-famous hugs. And my gratitude goes out to my parents, P.V. and Mary Chandy—for sacrificing, for coming along, for believing in me, and for believing in us.